AN INTRODUCTION TO THE NFL

Exhausted linemen from both teams put their hands on the ground, faced off against each other and prepared to summon up one last effort at the end of the longest Super Bowl in National Football League history. The San Francisco 49ers led the Kansas City Chiefs 22-19 as they moved towards the end of overtime in Las Vegas. The winner of the epic contest would be crowned champions of the NFL's 2023 season.

More than 60,000 fans inside Allegiant Stadium were screaming loud enough to raise the roof off the domed building and hundreds of millions around the world were glued to their television screens watching sporting history unfold before their very eyes.

Legendary Chiefs quarterback Patrick Mahomes received the ball at San Francisco's three-yard line, faked to hand it to running back Jerick McKinnon, before moving to his right and throwing the game-winning touchdown pass to Mecole Hardman.

Super Bowl 58 was over and the Kansas City Chiefs were NFL champions for the second year in a row! What followed next looked like something out of a classic sports movie. Mahomes leapt into Hardman's arms before disappearing under a pile of red-shirted bodies. Up in the stands, Taylor Swift – girlfriend of Chiefs tight end Travis Kelce – was also celebrating like crazy.

Mahomes then took off on a full sprint behind the end zone, reaching his own team bench and collapsing to the floor in a pile of joy, relief and exhaustion as red and gold confetti rained down on him from above. Players and coaches on the 49ers bench looked sick with grief as their championship dreams were ripped away from them in a split second. Every human emotion was on display on that historic night in Nevada.

Just under a year later, Mahomes and the Chiefs felt that same raw emotion from the other side of the equation. The superstar quarterback played one of the worst games of his career in Super Bowl 59 as Kansas City were soundly beaten 40-22 by the Philadelphia Eagles.

In a raucous Superdome in New Orleans, Mahomes was hit time and again by Philadelphia's dominant defensive line and bullied into several key mistakes as the Chiefs fell short of becoming the first team to win three Super Bowls in a row. This time around, the falling confetti was green and white as the Eagles were confirmed as champions of the 2024 NFL season. And the tears from Mahomes fell in frustration and despair, not as a result of glorious victory.

What a difference a year makes!

Those highs and lows experienced by Mahomes and the Chiefs during the 2023 and 2024 campaigns are typical of the NFL. It is an unpredictable league in a fast-paced, action-packed sport that serves up headline after headline, week after week and year after year.

As your NFL knowledge grows - through this book and by watching games yourself - you will quickly realise that the sport of American football - and its premier league - offers something for everyone.

Tune in to any game and you are likely to witness outstanding examples of grace and skill as quarterbacks fire 50-yard passes downfield to be reeled in by sprinting receivers or running backs weaving through a sea of bodies to score a touchdown. But there are also tremendous examples of physicality as defenders regularly make big tackles on opposing ball-carriers.

Tactics are also a huge part of American football and the result is an explosive, high-stakes game of chess with coaches looking to deceive each other with a series of moves and counter-moves.

The NFL will also appeal to fans who dream of success for their favourite team, no matter their form the

NFL

The Ultimate
Fan's Guide

For Poppy, the biggest Jags fan I know!

Love you, darling.
xxx

Neil Reynolds

NFL

The Ultimate
Fan's Guide

EBURY
PRESS

Ebury Press

UK | USA | Canada | Ireland | Australia
India | New Zealand | South Africa

Ebury Press is part of the Penguin Random House group
of companies whose addresses can be found at
global.penguinrandomhouse.com

Penguin Random House UK
One Embassy Gardens, 8 Viaduct Gardens, London SW11 7BW

penguin.co.uk
global.penguinrandomhouse.com

First published by Ebury Press in 2025
2

Typeset in 8.5/12.5pt Custer RE by Six Red Marbles UK,
Thetford, Norfolk

Printed and bound in Great Britain by Clays Ltd, Elcograf S.p.A.

The authorised representative in the EEA is Penguin Random House
Ireland, Morrison Chambers, 32 Nassau Street, Dublin D02 YH68

A CIP catalogue record for this book is available
from the British Library

ISBN 9781529960693

Penguin Random House is committed to a sustainable future
for our business, our readers and our planet. This book is made
from Forest Stewardship Council® certified paper.

An Introduction to the NFL

previous year. One of the most famous Hollywood depictions of American football is a 1999 film starring Al Pacino called *Any Given Sunday*. This film was named after the idea that no matter how dominant a team might appear on the surface, the competitive balance in the NFL means that all teams need to bring their A-game every single week.

The NFL has robust systems in place to ensure competitive balance and the results are clear to see. Over the past 17 seasons, the NFL has seen 12 different teams crowned champions. During that period, the only repeat title winners have been the New England Patriots, the Kansas City Chiefs and the Philadelphia Eagles – the parity among teams means there is more drama and excitement for fans.

Here's how the NFL creates a level playing field for its 32 teams.

THE SALARY CAP

There can be no domination of the transfer market or the building of super-teams in the NFL. Since 1994, the league has operated under a salary cap, which means each club has the same amount of money to spend on player wages. In 2025, each team is allowed to spend $279.2 million on its 53-man roster. If a team over-spends, they will be hit with financial penalties and/or lose draft picks. A team cannot sit on its money either. League rules stipulate that each franchise must spend at least 89 per cent of its cap over a four-year period.

REVENUE SHARING

Every club is on a strong financial footing due to the league's revenue-sharing model. All television deals and league-wide sponsorship – along with 40 per cent of a club's ticket sales – goes into one collective pot and is split evenly among the 32 franchises. All proceeds from merchandise sales are also evenly split. So, even if the Dallas Cowboys sell 20 million t-shirts and the Green Bay Packers sell one, that money is shared. The only money teams keep for themselves is 60 per cent of their ticket sales, gameday concessions and local sponsorships.

THE NFL DRAFT

You will hear more about the NFL Draft later, but this is a hugely impactful way the NFL levels its playing field. Every April, teams pick the leading college football players from across the United States to bolster their rosters. And they go worst to first. The club with the poorest record in the league gets to choose the best player coming out of college, all the way down to the reigning Super Bowl champions, who pick last. That order is repeated over seven rounds, allowing weaker teams to close the talent gap on the leading pack.

League Structure and Season

NFL STRUCTURE

There are 32 teams in the National Football League, split into eight divisions across two conferences. Half the league plays in four divisions in the AFC (American Football Conference) – the AFC East, AFC North, AFC South and AFC West. The other 16 teams make up the NFC (National Football Conference) and feature four clubs per division in the NFC East, NFC North, NFC South and NFC West.

Divisions are geographic by their nature. For example, the AFC East features the Buffalo Bills, Miami Dolphins, New England Patriots and New York Jets. All teams on America's east coast. By contrast, the NFC West features the Arizona Cardinals, Los Angeles Rams, San Francisco 49ers and Seattle Seahawks. All are situated out west.

National Football League

AMERICAN FOOTBALL CONFERENCE				NATIONAL FOOTBALL CONFERENCE			
AFC East	AFC North	AFC South	AFC West	NFC East	NFC North	NFC South	NFC West
Buffalo Bills	Baltimore Ravens	Houston Texans	Denver Broncos	Dallas Cowboys	Chicago Bears	Atlanta Falcons	Arizona Cardinals
Miami Dolphins	Cincinnati Bengals	Indianapolis Colts	Kansas City Chiefs	New York Giants	Detroit Lions	Carolina Panthers	Los Angeles Rams
New England Patriots	Cleveland Browns	Jacksonville Jaguars	Las Vegas Raiders	Philadelphia Eagles	Green Bay Packers	New Orleans Saints	San Francisco 49ers
New York Jets	Pittsburgh Steelers	Tennessee Titans	Los Angeles Chargers	Washington Commanders	Minnesota Vikings	Tampa Bay Buccaneers	Seattle Seahawks

NFL SCHEDULE

Each team plays 17 league games over 18 weeks from September to early January. Under the NFL scheduling formula, fixtures are arranged as follows:

— **Home and away against the other three teams in their division (six games).**

— **Four teams from another division within their conference on a rotating three-year cycle (four games). For example, in the 2025 season (which will stretch into the early part of 2026) the Jacksonville Jaguars will play the teams from AFC West: Denver Broncos, Kansas City Chiefs, Las Vegas Raiders and Los Angeles Chargers.**

— **Four teams from a division from the other conference on a rotating four-year cycle (four games). For example, in 2025, the Jacksonville Jaguars will play teams from NFC West: Arizona Cardinals, Los Angeles Rams, San Francisco 49ers and Seattle Seahawks.**

— **Two teams from the same conference who placed in the same position in their respective divisions, providing they are not already scheduled to meet. First place finisher versus first place finisher, for example (two games). As the Jacksonville Jaguars finished 3rd in the AFC South in 2024, they will play New York Jets (who finished 3rd in AFC East) and Cincinnati Bengals (who finished 3rd in AFC North).**

— **One additional team from the other conference that finished in the same position as them (one game). In 2025, the Jacksonville Jaguars will play the Carolina Panthers, as both teams finished 3rd in their divisions in 2024.**

NFC

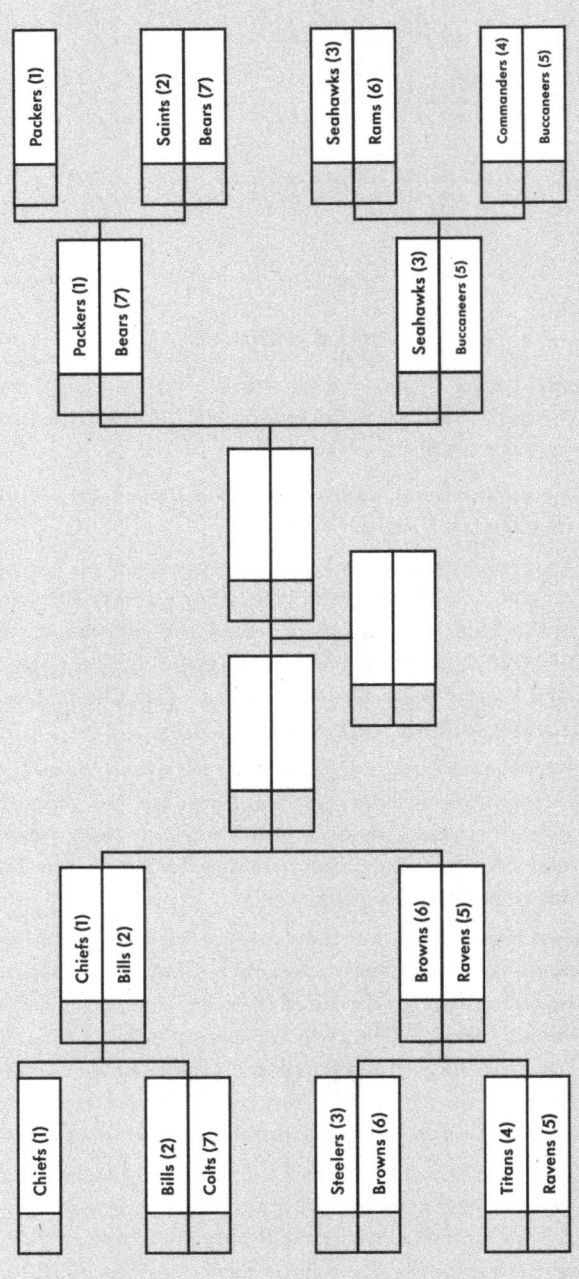

AFC

THE PLAYOFFS

The leading seven AFC teams (four division winners and three franchises with the next-best records, known as Wild Card teams) will qualify for the playoffs. They will then compete in a knockout competition in January with the champion of the AFC reaching the Super Bowl. That formula is repeated in the NFC – seven playoff qualifiers, a knockout tournament and an eventual NFC champion to advance to the Super Bowl.

There is only one prize in the NFL. There are no cup competitions – the winner of the Super Bowl, played each February, is crowned the league's champion. Prior to the birth of the Super Bowl in the 1966 season, the NFL still found a way to name a league champion. From 1920 to 1932, there were no playoff games and the league champion was the team with the best winning percentage, excluding ties. As teams would often play varying numbers of games and against various levels of talent, the first four league champions were disputed and had to be determined by the NFL's executive committee. From 1933 to 1965, the NFL played a single title game to crown its champion before it morphed into the Super Bowl we know today.

Former Pro Bowl (the NFL's all-star game that sees players voted in by fellow pros, coaches and fans) cornerback Josh Norman explains: 'It's not like you have four different divisions where you can win all these trophies and claim to be king of the mountaintop. No, this is like the FIFA World Cup – there's just one. The grandaddy of them all is the Super Bowl and that's the prize we're after.'

The Basics

THE BASICS

Like all sports, American football has many rules and nuances. But you don't need to know all of them right away. Here are some basics to get you started on your gridiron journey.

THE TEAMS

Each NFL squad carries 53 players on their roster, although only 11 can be on the field at any one time. There are unlimited substitutions throughout an NFL game.

THE PITCH

An NFL field is 100 yards from goal-line to goal-line and 53.3 yards wide. At each end of the pitch is a 10-yard scoring area known as the end zone.

THE CLOCK

Each game features 60 minutes of playing time, spread over four 15-minute quarters. There is a halftime break after the second quarter and the game resumes with a kick-off after a break–this is typically 13 minutes but stretches to more than 20 minutes in the Super Bowl to accommodate the famous halftime show. At the end of the first and third quarters, play continues where it left off once the teams have changed ends. Factoring in clock stoppages (there are times when the clock can stop due to a pass falling incomplete or a player running out of bounds), an average NFL game lasts just over three hours.

CHAPTER 03

MOVING THE BALL

The attacking team – the offense – moves the ball in a series of plays called downs. The offense can choose to run the ball or the quarterback can throw to a teammate. Each down ends when the ball-carrier is tackled to the ground or a pass falls incomplete and hits the ground without being caught.

The offense aims to gain 10 yards in four plays to keep possession and earn a fresh set of downs, while the defense fights to disrupt that plan. Here is an example of how a series of plays might unfold.

— 1st and 10 at Offense 20-yard line   Run for 3 yards.

This means it is first down for the offense and they have 10 yards to go before they earn a new set of downs. The ball being on the offense's 20-yard line means it is 20 yards from their own end zone and 80 yards away from their opponent's end zone.

— 2nd and 7 at Offense 23-yard line	Incomplete pass
— 3rd and 7 at Offense 23-yard line	Pass completion for 10 yards
— 1st and 10 at Offense 33-yard line	Pass completion for 20 yards
— 1st and 10 at Opponent 47-yard line	Run for 5 yards
— 2nd and 5 at Opponent 42-yard line	Incomplete pass
— 3rd and 5 at Opponent 42-yard line	Pass completion for 22 yards
— 1st and 10 at Opponent 20-yard line	Incomplete pass
— 2nd and 10 at Opponent 20-yard line	Run for 18 yards
— 1st and Goal at Opponent 2-yard line	Pass completion for 2 yards – Touchdown!

If the offense fails to gain 10 yards in four plays, they give up the ball at the spot of their failure. So, in reality, teams have three downs to gain 10 yards because, on fourth down, they will typically punt the ball away to the opposition (playing for territory) or attempt a kick at goal if within range. That said, if a team is feeling aggressive or if they are in good field position, there are occasions where they will run another traditional play on fourth down in an attempt to keep the ball for themselves. If they fail, the other team takes possession of the ball at the spot where theprevious play ended.

If the ball is thrown and falls to the ground without being caught, the clock stops and there is no gain on the play. So, if the quarterback throws what is known as an incomplete pass, first down and 10 becomes second down and 10.

SCORING

Touchdown = 6 points

Scored when a player crosses the opponent's goal-line with the ball or catches the ball in the end zone. Despite the name, the ball does not need to be touched down.

Extra Point = 1 point

Earned after a touchdown by kicking the ball over the crossbar and through the uprights from 33 yards, similar to a rugby conversion.

Two-point conversion = 2 points

Added after a touchdown by the offense taking the ball into the end zone again – via a run or pass – from the two-yard line. This is essentially just another normal play.

Field Goal = 3 points

Usually attempted on fourth down if the kicker is within range of the posts. His kick must go over the crossbar and between the posts.

Safety = 2 points

Awarded to the defense when they tackle an offensive player with the ball in his own end zone. This is essentially American football's version of an own goal in soccer. For example, the offense may have the ball at their own one-yard line and the running back – who lines up four or five yards behind the quarterback – could receive the ball in his own end zone. If he is tackled to the ground before escaping his own end zone, that is a safety. Or, the quarterback could retreat away from the one-yard line to throw downfield. If he is tackled in his own end zone, that is known as a sack and, again, would result in the two-point safety.

The Positions

THE POSITIONS

As mentioned in the previous chapter, each NFL team carries 53 players on its roster, with 48 of those being active on each match day. With unlimited substitutions throughout an NFL game, players come on and off the field as many times as required. They do not stay on the pitch performing multiple roles, as can be the case in other sports like soccer and rugby. An American football team is made up of three specialised and separate units known as the offense, defense and special teams.

THE OFFENSE

The job of the offense is simple – to move downfield by either running or passing the football and to score points. Here are the key positions for an NFL offense.

Offensive Line

The wall of muscle known as the offensive line features five players who perform a vital role. An NFL team could have the brightest stars at other positions, but it will all come crashing down without good blocking up front. The middle of the line features a center, who passes the ball between his legs to the quarterback in order to start each play. This is known as a snap. The two men either side of the center are powerfully built guards and the two blockers on the edge of the line are more athletic tackles, designed to deal with speedy defenders trying to get to the quarterback. On running plays, the line will power forward and block defenders in a bid to open space for the running back. When this group drops back to form a protective shield

THE OFFENSE

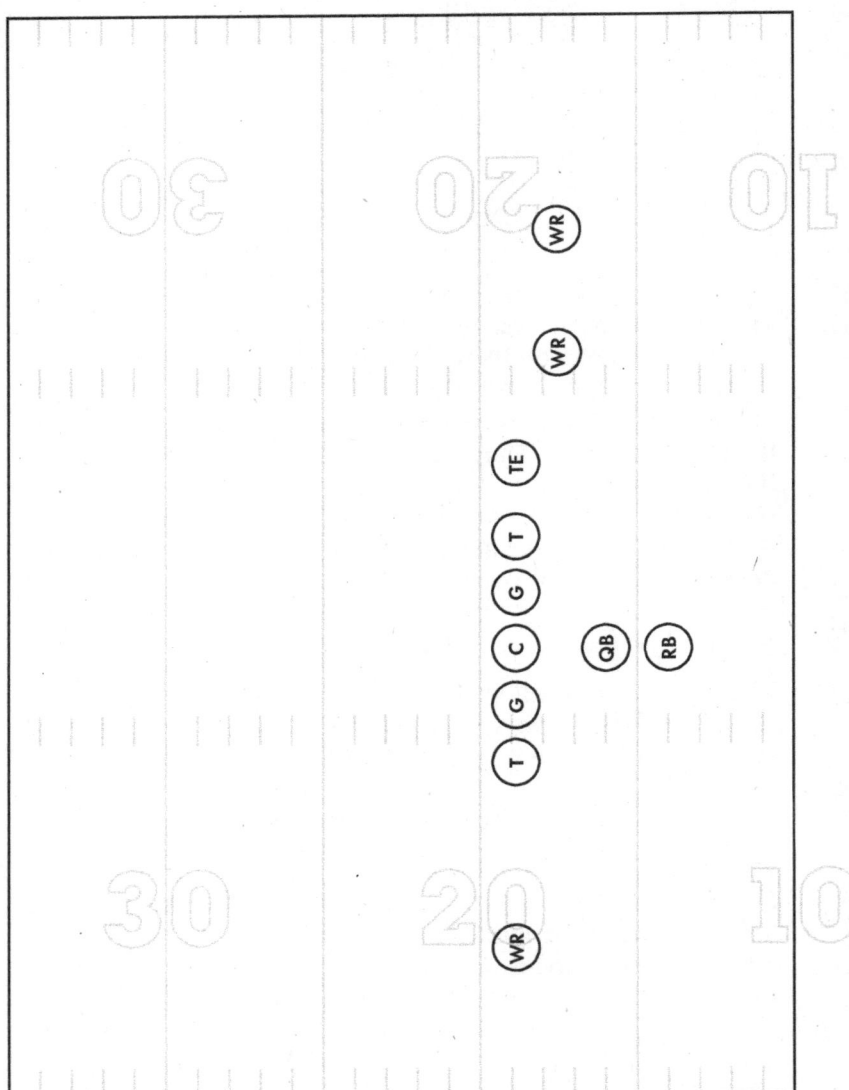

KEY
— T = Tackle (part of the Offensive Line)
— G = Guard (part of the Offensive Line)
— C = Center (part of the Offensive Line)
— QB = Quarterback
— RB = Running Back
— WR = Wide Receiver
— TE = Tight End

around the quarterback (known as a pocket), it's most likely to be a pass downfield.

Quarterback

The quarterback is the golden boy of the NFL and plays American football's most vital position. If you have one of the league's better quarterbacks, you have a shot at Super Bowl glory. If you don't have an established player at this position, your team is going to be in trouble! The Kansas City Chiefs are the perfect example of that logic. Since Patrick Mahomes became their full-time starter in 2018, they have reached at least the semi-final stage of the Super Bowl race in every season. They have played in five Super Bowls and have won three since 2019.

The quarterback touches the ball on every play. After receiving the snap from the center, the quarterback has two options. . .

Option one: Passing play

— **On a passing play, the quarterback throws the ball to a receiver. Today's NFL teams tend to pass the ball more than they run it, placing that emphasis on the quarterback to be an effective player.**

Option two: Running play

— **On a running play, the quarterback hands the ball to his teammate, who runs upfield or runs the ball themselves towards the end zone.**

For more information on the options that the quarterback has, see Chapter 5.

Quarterbacks are the highest-paid players in the NFL, with the best earning up to $60 million per year, but they earn their money by playing what is often described as the toughest position in all of sports. When setting to throw, a quarterback must assess how the opposition is defending the play, scan the entire field to find an open receiver, and deliver an inch-perfect throw – often to an area his teammate will run into moments later – while an angry 300-pound monster barrels ever closer, determined to deliver a big hit. And all of that must ideally be accomplished within two and a half to four seconds.

'You have to be on it on every single play,' says Miami Dolphins quarterback Tua Tagovailoa. 'You have to know what everyone on the field is doing – all 11 guys on your side, all 11 guys on the other side, and there are a lot of things that go into the quarterback position.'

The greatest quarterback of all time – seven-time Super Bowl champion Tom Brady – believes keeping a clear head is vital for the position, as he explains: 'There are a lot of distractions you have to block out. You have to make sure everybody is calm and no one is freaking out or getting too excited. You kind of have to play a little counsellor, a little coach and a little quarterback. That's the fun part and that's what we sign up for.'

Quarterbacks come with varying skills. Some excel at throwing strong passes (Buffalo's Josh Allen), others shine through their accuracy and decision-making (Cincinnati's Joe Burrow); and then there are those who rely heavily on their athleticism to evade defenders and run downfield like a running back (Baltimore's Lamar Jackson). Those who can combine all of those skills and deliver in the biggest of moments are among the best in the game today, with Mahomes leading the way.

HIGHEST-PAID NFL QUARTERBACKS – AS OF 1 APRIL 2025

— DAK PRESCOTT	DALLAS COWBOYS	$60M PER YEAR
— JOSH ALLEN	BUFFALO BILLS	$55M PER YEAR
— JOE BURROW	CINCINNATI BENGALS	$55M PER YEAR
— TREVOR LAWRENCE	JACKSONVILLE JAGUARS	$55M PER YEAR
— JORDAN LOVE	GREEN BAY PACKERS	$55M PER YEAR

Running Back

The running back is one of the NFL's most versatile players. Lined up in the backfield behind or to the side of the quarterback, he must be able to run, catch and block. There are many different types of running backs in the NFL. Some excel through speed (De'Von Achane, of the Miami Dolphins), some due to their vision and ability to pick a soft spot in the defense (Chuba Hubbard, of the Carolina Panthers) and others who have an array of spins and hurdles that make them tough to bring down (Saquon Barkley, of the Philadelphia Eagles). And then there are those who get by on brute force, using their physicality to take the fight to the defenders (Derrick Henry, of the Baltimore Ravens). And the very best in the game can do all of the above.

Wide Receiver

The wide receiver is the speedster of the offense whose job is to get downfield as quickly as possible and catch passes from the quarterback. While those like Tyreek Hill, of the Miami Dolphins, boast sprinter's speed, slower receivers can still be useful if they have an ability to separate from defenders and find space to receive the throw. And big-bodied receivers also have a value as they can use their physicality to get into perfect position and win jump balls with smaller defenders trying to cover them. A receiver who can do all of those things is extremely valuable to his team, which is why Ja'Marr Chase, of the Cincinnati Bengals, is the highest-paid non-quarterback in the NFL, with an annual salary of $40.25 million.

Tight End

This hybrid player sets up on the end of the offensive line or in the space between the line and the wide receiver. The tight end can be asked to block defenders on running plays so they cannot tackle the running back advancing downfield with the ball. But when it is a passing play, he runs downfield and presents a bigger and more physical target for the quarterback. The tight end is often best suited to exploit weaknesses in a defense, as he can be too fast for some defenders and too big for others.

THE DEFENSE

A defense is built on three levels – the line, the linebackers and the defensive backs (cornerbacks and safeties). The aim of the defense is to stop the offense from gaining yards and scoring points. Here are the key positions.

Defensive End/Edge Rusher

These defenders line up on each end of the line and have a massive role to play in the pass-happy NFL. Defensive ends – also known as edge rushers – are more athletic than defensive linemen, who operate towards the middle of the line - and while they will tackle running backs when required to do so, their primary role is to be in attack mode. These are the men tasked with making life as difficult as possible for opposing quarterbacks, cutting off passes downfield at source. Either tackling the quarterback before he throws the football – which is known as a sack – or pressuring the quarterback into an inaccurate throw can seriously impact an offense's passing attack. Edge rushers Myles Garrett, of the Cleveland Browns, Las Vegas Raiders star Maxx Crosby, and Nick Bosa, of the San Francisco 49ers, were the highest-paid defenders in the NFL as of 1 April 2025, stressing the importance of this position.

Defensive Tackle

The role of a defensive tackle can vary, depending on the type of defense he plays in. Some teams will play two defensive tackles in a four-man line and these players will be tasked with defending the run but also with pressuring the quarterback. The best in the game at this is Kansas City's Chris Jones, who is one of the highest-paid defenders in the league, earning more than $31 million per season. Other teams will play just one defensive tackle – also referred to as a nose tackle because he lines up right in the center's face. This defender can often be an unsung hero, occupying blockers so teammates behind him can run free to make key tackles.

THE 4-3 DEFENSE

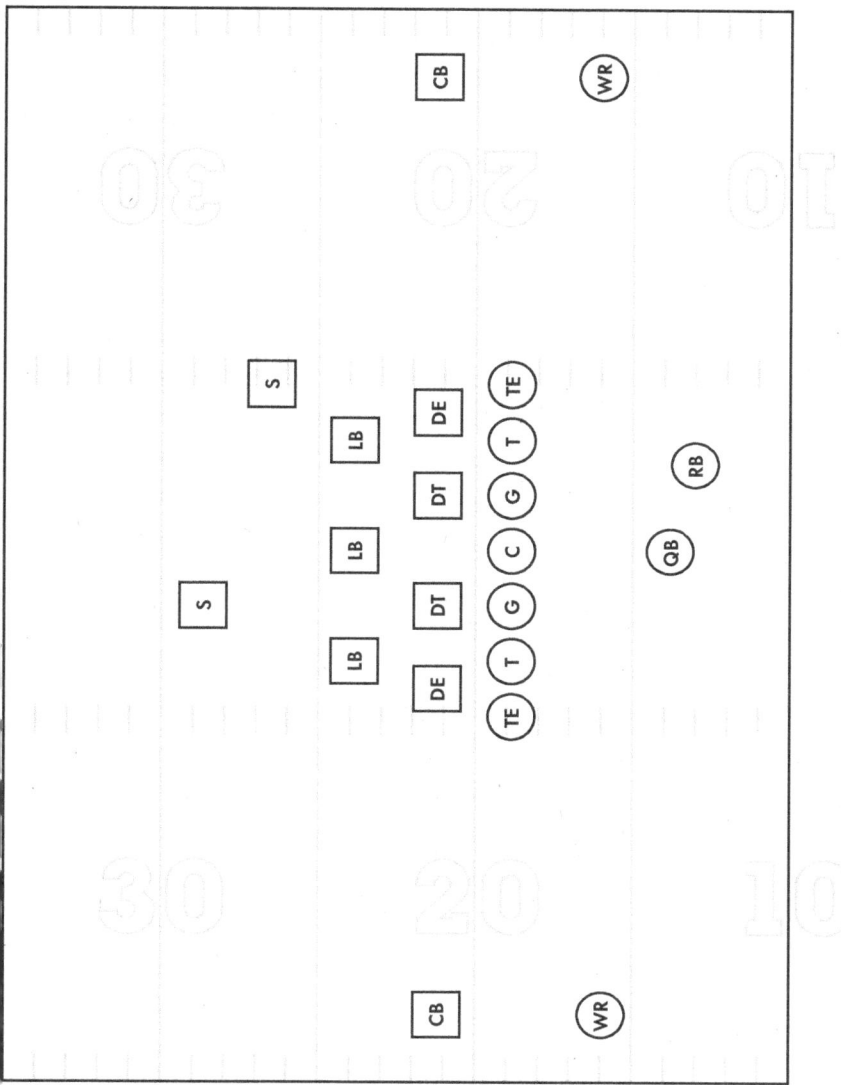

KEY

- T = Tackle (part of the Offensive Line)
- G = Guard (part of the Offensive Line)
- C = Center (part of the Offensive Line)
- QB = Quarterback
- RB = Running Back
- WR = Wide Receiver
- TE = Tight End

- DE = Defensive End
- DT = Defensive Tackle
- LB = Linebacker
- CB = Cornerback
- S = Safety

THE 3-4 DEFENSE

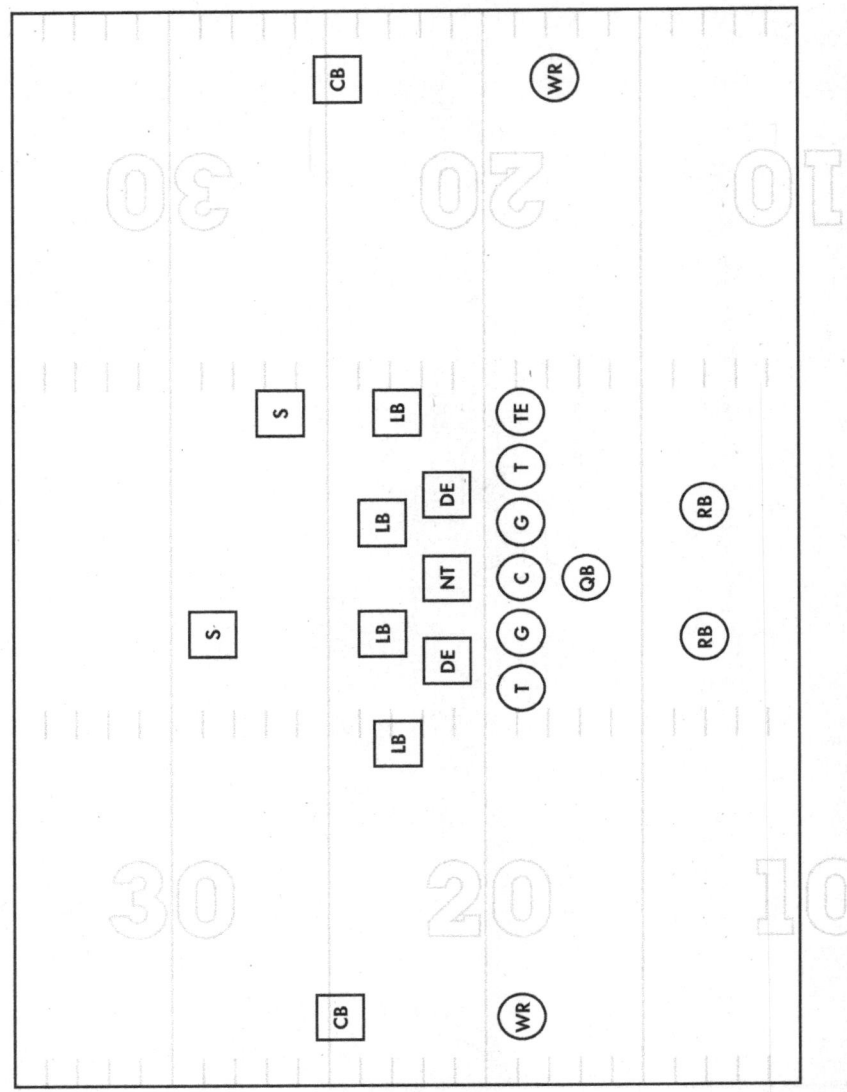

KEY
- T = Tackle (part of the Offensive Line)
- G = Guard (part of the Offensive Line)
- C = Center (part of the Offensive Line)
- QB= Quarterback
- RB = Running Back
- WR = Wide Receiver
- TE = Tight End

- DE = Defensive End
- NT = Nose Tackle
- LB = Linebacker
- CB = Cornerback
- S = Safety

THE POSITIONS

Linebackers

These hybrid defenders do a little bit of everything. When the offense runs the ball, the linebacker must evade or fight off blockers, track the running back and then secure the tackle. When the quarterback retreats away from the line to throw, the linebacker can be used in two ways - he can drop back and cover one of the slower-moving passing targets, such as the tight end or the running back, or he can be sent running straight towards the quarterback as an additional surprise pass rusher. This is known as a blitz.

Cornerback

The cornerback marks the offense's fastest and nimblest players - the wide receivers. There can be anywhere between two and four cornerbacks on the field, depending on the situation, and their job is to mirror the movements of the receiver and move at high speed, quite often while running backwards! The cornerback must disrupt the receiver and not allow him to make a catch. A real bonus for the defense comes when the cornerback catches the quarterback's throw - this is known as an interception and gives possession of the ball back to his offense.

Safety

As the name of the position would suggest, a team's two safeties are the last line of defense. If a safety misses a tackle, the result is often a touchdown for the other team. A good safety will be versatile - stopping the run, covering receivers and tight ends, and reading the quarterback's eyes before pouncing for a vital interception.

SPECIAL TEAMS

This group features a lot of existing players from offense and defense who are called into action in kicking and change-of-possession situations. But there are also some very important specialists.

Kicker

The kicker handles kick-offs and all kicks at goal – field goals and extra points. The kicker does not play another position and could be a virtual spectator for three hours, but his boot can win or lose games, so being able to handle pressure is a must.

Punter

This is the one player fans never want to see because he features at the end of offensive failure. The punter's job on fourth down is to kick for territory and to send the ball as high and as far down the other end of the field as possible.

Long-Snapper

The long-snapper is charged with getting the ball back to the kicker and punter as quickly as possible (ideally within ¾ of a second) by throwing it between his legs. He then protects as a blocker on kicks at goal or races downfield to make tackles on punts.

Holder

Catching from the long-snapper, the holder must place the ball on the ground – with the laces away from the kicker – for all kicks at goal. A bad catch or hold can result in a missed field goal, as precision timing is vital in these pressure situations.

Kick and Punt Returners

A return man is normally a wide receiver, running back or cornerback with a mix of speed and elusive moves. His job is to run the ball as far back upfield as possible after fielding a kick-off or a punt.

Advanced Tactics

Okay, so now that you have an idea of American football's rules and positions, it's time to dig a little deeper and to explore some of the tactics in what is often described as a fast, action-packed game of chess.

And to guide us through some of those strategic battles – often referred to as X's and O's - is NFL Academy head coach Steve Hagen, who coached 11 years in the NFL with the Cleveland Browns and New York Jets, as well as at some of America's leading colleges before taking up his role with the NFL's international high-school programme based in Loughborough.

MANAGING THE GAME . . .

One of the pillars of our programme here is 'never flinch.' You have to balance your emotions. There are times when you just want to say 'Let's go' and be aggressive. But you have to be pragmatic and wonder how the situation is going to end up. As a coach, you've constantly got to have a foot on the gas and a foot on the brake. You're constantly adjusting. It may sound crazy, but American football is very much like military strategy. If we deploy this, what do they do? And if they do this, how do we counter that? American football is very unique – you have to get your guys to fight in controlled chaos.

BEFORE THE SNAP . . .

Personnel and Formations . . .

Personnel creates a mismatch. For example, we may be in 12 personnel (one running back and two tight ends). If we get two big tight ends on the field, we can catch the defense because our tight end might be better than the linebacker they have been designated to cover. That's a way to get a strategic mismatch. You may have (Hall of Fame wide receiver) Randy Moss out there, so the defense puts a fast little cornerback on the field. On your next play you go to 12 personnel, with two big tight ends, and if that little cornerback is still out there, you go and attack him. We can do the same formation with every personnel group, but the defense can't defend it as well and they get trapped in. They may have little guys on the field and we will put the big guys out there, but have them in a spread formation. They spread out with us and then we run the ball with our more powerful players on the field. You're always trying to create mismatches.

MOVING YOUR PLAYERS . . .

Motion is the movement of a player – a wide receiver, tight end or running back – from one side of the formation to the other before the snap. If you motion or shift somebody, that opens up possible advantages. So, in an NFL game, you will see formation, motion and shifts and personnel all playing a role at the same time. It can get confusing for a defense if they're not prepared for it. Then you will get them into a check mode, which means they will say, 'If the offense does this, we're just going to do this.' When you watch videos of your opponents, also known as film, throughout the week before the game, you can figure out how they react to specific situations on the field. As an offense you can know that if you get into a certain personnel group, the defense will check to a certain formation or coverage. And then we can call a specific play based off that and we have the advantage. We're looking to see how their defense adjusts to our motion. Motion also absolutely tells us about the coverages the defense is going to run. Are they going to leave the middle of the field open or close the middle of the field with their safeties? When they do that, we know how to attack both those situations. If we send a guy in motion and they rotate their safeties to a certain side of the field in coverage the way we anticipate, if we have the right play called, it can be very dynamic.

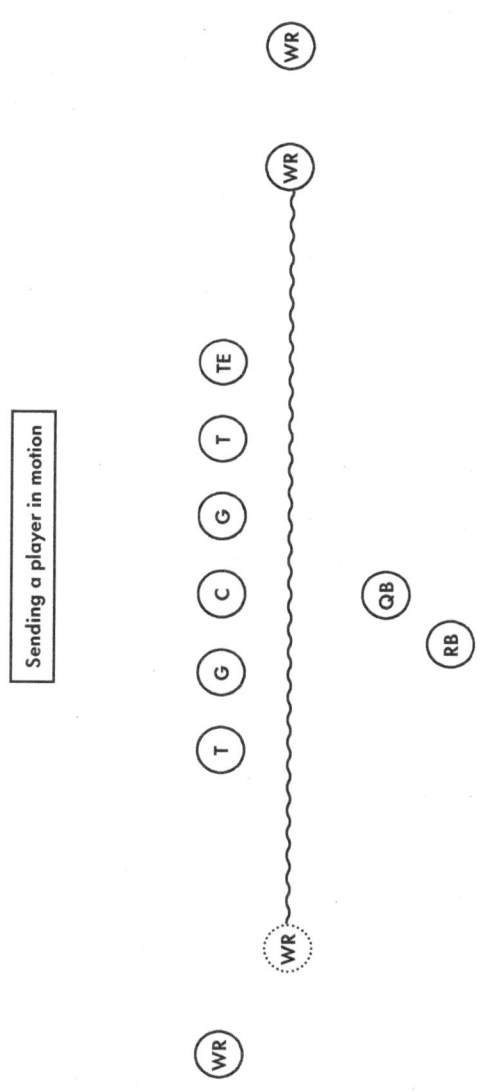

Sending a player in motion

KEY
- T = Tackle (part of the Offensive Line)
- G = Guard (part of the Offensive Line)
- C = Center (part of the Offensive Line)
- QB = Quarterback
- RB = Running Back
- WR = Wide Receiver
- TE = Tight End

The Quarterback's Reads . . .

Whether it be in the NFL, in college football or here at the NFL Academy, these are three initial reads a quarterback has to make.

Pre-snap . . .

The first job is that pre-snap, first wide vision of all 11 players on his team. That's to see if our team is lined up right – we have to make sure we're in the right formation. There are a lot of plays, guys are coming in and out and there is a lot of action before the snap. 'Are all of us right? Okay, good.'

Reading the defense . . .

Second wide vision is, 'Are the defense lined up the way we anticipate them to be?' That comes through constant film study. If we have two receivers on each side, are they lined up how we think they should be? They may not be. They may uncover the inside receiver on the right. And that takes us to the third piece. Where are they at a disadvantage? They may not be. That's when we motion and we can create an advantage for ourselves. First wide vision, us. Second wide vision, them.

Do we have the right play? . . .

Third wide vision: 'Are we in the best play to attack what they're defending us with?' If it is, we run the play. If not, let's audible (call out a new set of instructions at the line of scrimmage) to another play. If we run the play, there are sight adjustments within that if they blitz or do something unexpected.

PASSING THE BALL...

On this or any passing play, the primary target can vary based on a number of factors, such as . . . who has the best chance of getting open due to the play's design, the coverage being presented by the defense, and even who is in form or is the offense's best player.

There are typically five receivers in every route and they all have a job to do. They go to reception areas on the field and the quarterback has those memorised. The quarterback can say, 'Based on this coverage, we expect this to happen so you will get into this reception area on time and I will be able to throw the ball on target.' That's when you might hear pundits on TV talking about an offense having great timing – that's because the anticipated reception area is getting filled with the right receiver at the correct time, so everything works well.

It's Good To Have Options . . .

It's not always as black and white as saying that a certain receiver runs here or there. If the defense goes outside of you, the receiver turns in. If they stay inside, the receiver turns out. If the defense covers your receivers man on man in a physical manner, you break in or out depending which way the defender favours. There are a lot of different options. We don't give everybody the option to adjust plans on the fly – we only give one or possibly two guys the option on a particular play. Otherwise, all five of them would be running all over the place. Usually, we'll give four guys the static routes and one guy the option. As well as primary options for the receivers, there will be a planned checkdown pass to the running back if nothing else is available. But the back doesn't always become available because he has to block defenders to protect his quarterback. Then the quarterback has to scramble (run) behind the line of scrimmage and look for an open receiver. That turns into scramble rules for receivers.

PASSING THE BALL . . .

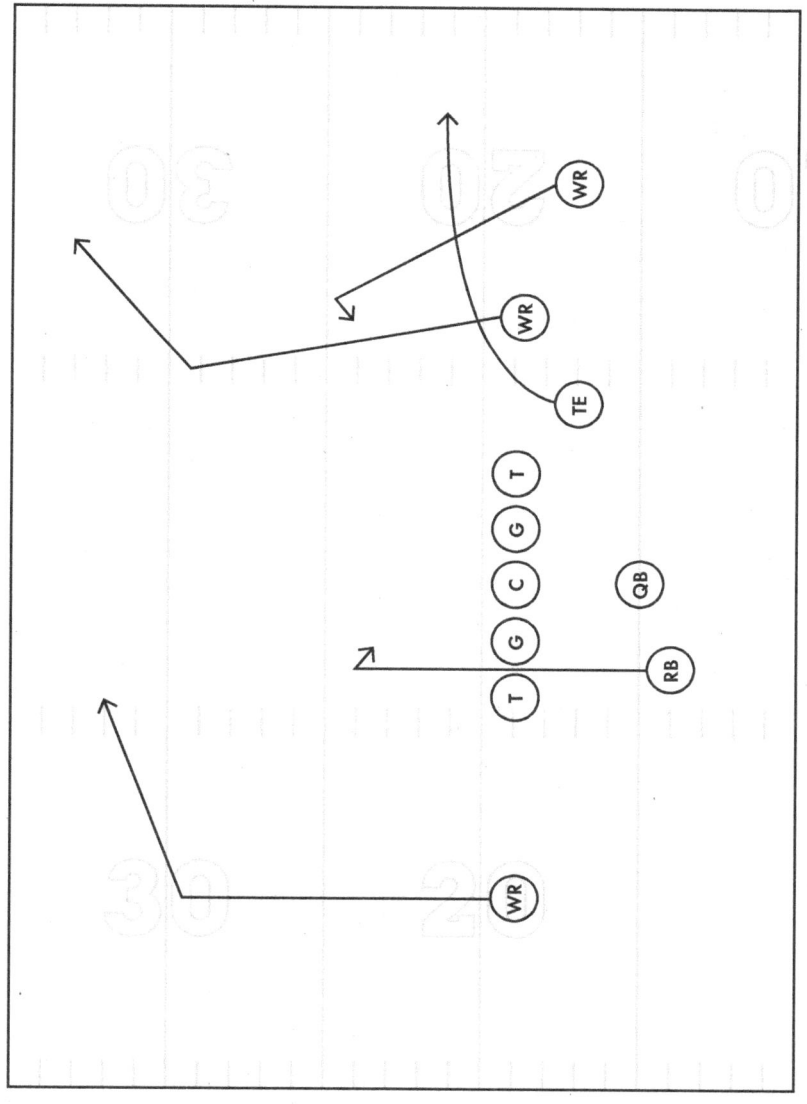

KEY
- T = Tackle (part of the Offensive Line)
- G = Guard (part of the Offensive Line)
- C = Center (part of the Offensive Line)
- QB= Quarterback
- RB = Running Back
- WR = Wide Receiver
- TE = Tight End

THERE SHOULD ALWAYS BE A PLAN B . . .

The rules for those scrambles would be that if the quarterback was running to his right and we had routes going left, the receivers have to put on their brakes, reverse the field and start running right. The deepest guy would take off and start running towards the back corner of the end zone, one of the guys on the left side has to run to the right flat and guys running down the sidelines have to come back to the quarterback. That extended action is a play within a play, because everybody has to adjust based on what they see in the moment and realise the quarterback is off his regular launch point behind the offensive line, he's broken out and he's extended the play, so the receivers now have to go with him. People call that chaos. . . we call it a play. There should never really be any chaos.

THERE SHOULD ALWAYS BE A PLAN B

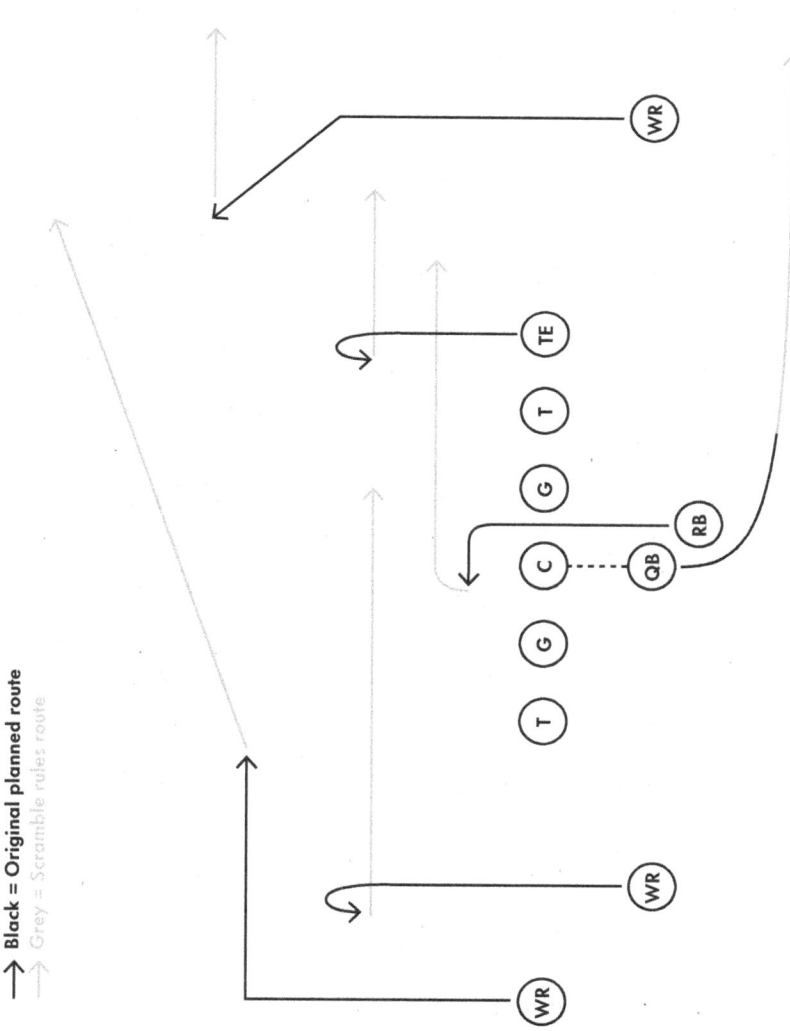

KEY
— T = Tackle (part of the Offensive Line)
— G = Guard (part of the Offensive Line)
— C = Center (part of the Offensive Line)
— QB= Quarterback
— RB = Running Back
— WR = Wide Receiver
— TE = Tight End

UNSELFISH PLAYERS WANTED . . .

All receivers are connected. Not all routes see every receiver as the primary target. They are designed to pull a defender so the primary receiver can get open in front of the deepest defenders or in the area towards the sidelines, which is known as the flat. On the play diagrammed below, Player Z is drawing the safety away so that Player X is in one-on-one coverage and can catch the pass across the middle. There is another option for the quarterback if Player X is not available. Player F is drawing the linebacker to the right side of the field. The quarterback can then throw to Player Y, who should be in one-on-one coverage heading to the left side of the field. So, on this play. . .

— **Z is creating an opportunity for X**
— **F is creating an opportunity for Y**

The quarterback would read high to low. . . so he would throw to Player X first, as that would gain the most yards. If not, he will throw to Player Y for a shorter gain of yardage. We might also put three receivers on one side of the formation to draw more defenders to that side of the field. Then we call a play for our lone receiver on the other side, who might be Randy Moss. Do we think Randy can beat this one-on-one coverage because the defense has concerned itself with three receivers on the other side? You will see the quarterback signal a play to that single receiver based on the coverage – it could be a wink or a tap of the helmet or thigh. That is all sight-adjusted between the quarterback and his receivers.

UNSELFISH PLAYERS WANTED

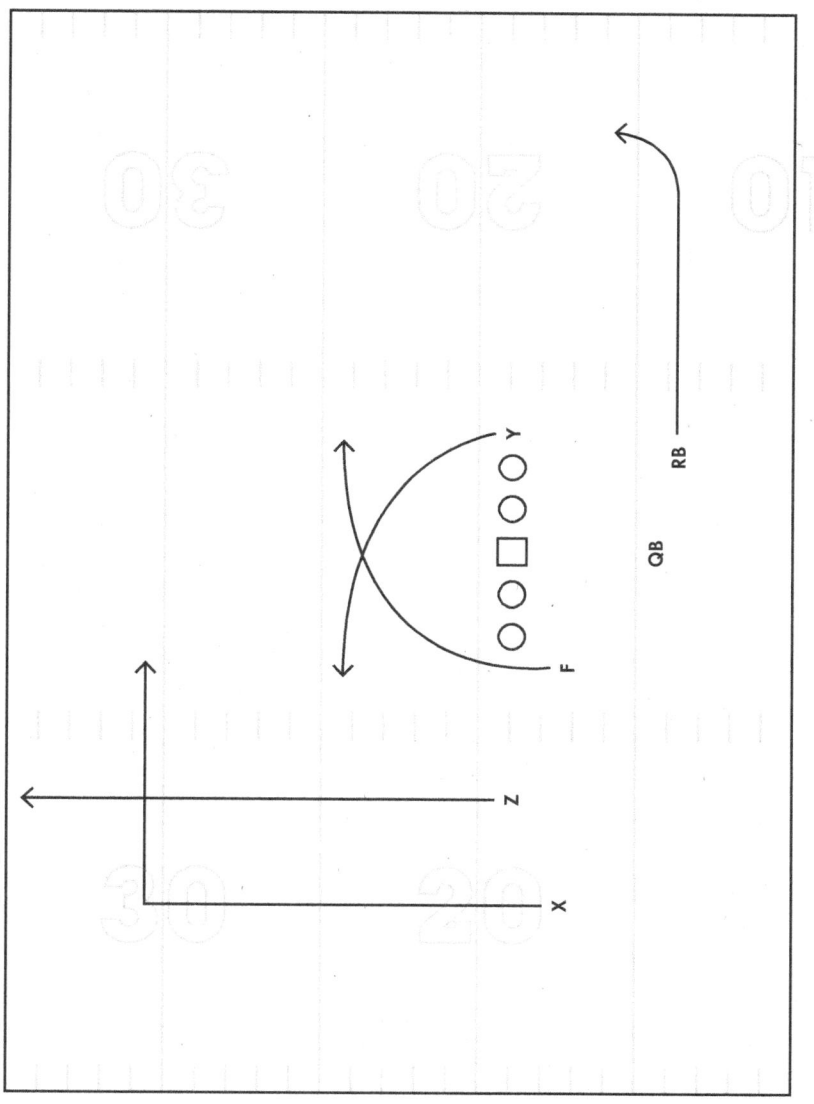

KEY
— Z (Wide Receiver 2) is creating an opportunity for X (Wide Reciever 1)
— F (Tight End 1) is creating an opportunity for Y (Tight End 2)

CHAPTER 05

RUNNING THE BALL . . .

Throughout an NFL season, you will find teams will either start to tackle better or. . . worse! That's because they're beaten up and injured or it could be that they're not winning and their heart isn't in it as much as it was at the front end of the season when they thought they were going to the Super Bowl. When you're on defense and you know you have no chance to go to the Super Bowl and it's getting cold and the hits are a little harder, that's tough. Football is a game of attrition and yardage and how you get those yards. And how you control time with the ball because, when you run, the clock doesn't stop. The most important thing about running the football is the physicality – you can impose your will on the defense. If you have a good running game, you will have a good team. That's where your game starts, with a good running attack, and then you build off that with those play-action passes.

The Play-Action Pass

In this play:

- **Quarterback fakes handling the ball to the Running Back.**
- **The Linebacker, Safety and Cornerback move forward to defend the run.**
- **This creates space over the top of the defense for Quarterback to throw the ball downfield.**

If you run the ball, you're going to attract attention from the defense in terms of stopping the runner. And to do that, they're taking people out of pass coverage to tackle that big, powerful running back, like a Derrick Henry (Baltimore Ravens). If he keeps running through the line, the defense has to get a safety to come down and help defend the run. And the linebackers have to be moving forward to stop the run. If you then fake giving the ball to Derrick Henry and you've got a receiver over the top where that safety was supposed to be (known as a play-action pass), that's a touchdown!

THE PLAY-ACTION PASS

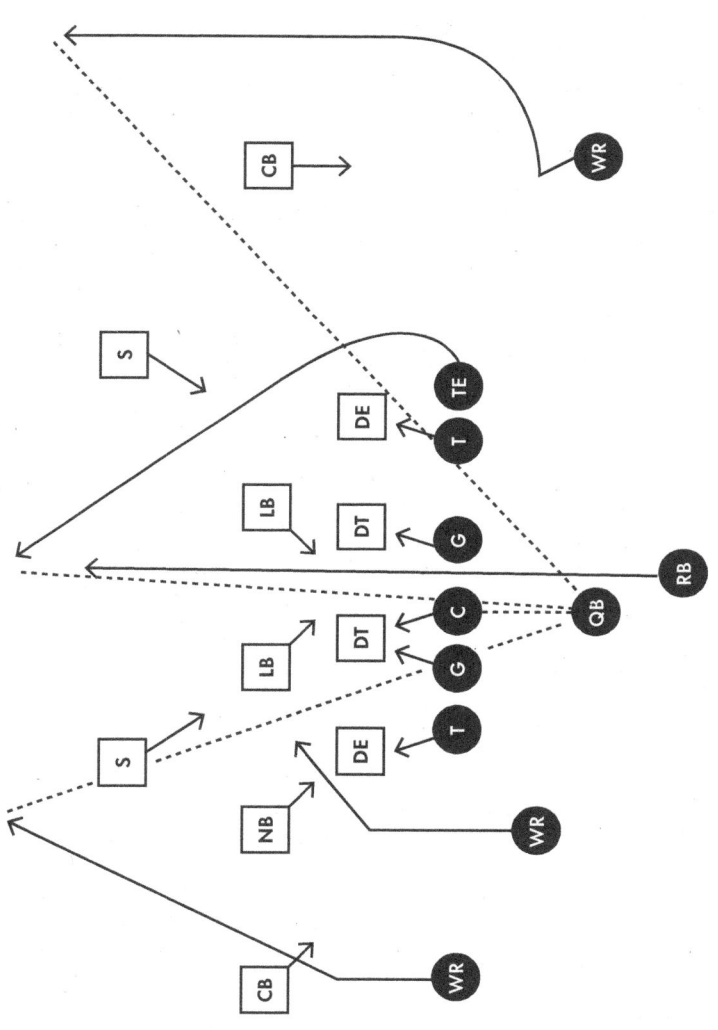

KEY
- T = Tackle (part of the Offensive Line)
- G = Guard (part of the Offensive Line)
- C = Centre (part of the Offensive Line)
- QB= Quarterback
- RB = Running back
- WR = Wide Receiver
- TE = Tight End
- DE = Defensive End
- NT = Nose Tackle
- LB = Linebacker
- CB = Cornerback
- S = Safety

ADJUSTING ON DEFENSE . . .

We will gather tendencies off film, and you have everything you need in terms of film at the NFL level. What's the percentage that the opponent likes to run the ball on first down? If it's 80 per cent, then we may have run blitzes for that. And do they run to a certain side 80 per cent of the time because they like a specific offensive lineman? You try to overload their gaps and bring secondary players down to help with the run. So, if we think a team is going to run a lot, we will bring defenders closer to the line to deal with that, and if we think they are going to pass more, we will put five or six faster defensive backs on the field. That's the chess match.

Play Fast and Smart . . .

Coaches have to process but players have to process too. At the NFL Academy, we say 'Smart, fast, physical, fundamental football players who do whatever it takes to win and leave no doubt.' The smarter you are, the faster you will play this game. The smarter you are, the more physical you will play this game. The smarter you are, the more you will play this game with good basic skills when it comes to blocking, tackling and executing your job correctly. We call these the fundamentals. You can be slower than your opponent, but when you're fundamentally sound and more physical, you will intimidate your opponent and the game will be over.

IT ALL COMES DOWN TO THIS . . .

What American football comes down to is this. . . can you or they play at quarterback? Do they have a quarterback who can win the game? When we would go into NFL games, it was not about an opponent having a vaunted defense. It was more a case of us saying, 'They've got Tom Brady on that side' or 'They have Drew Brees or Peyton Manning or Aaron Rodgers and we don't.' Then we have to play great defense and do all we can on offense. Those teams are always going to be in games. That's why those leading NFL quarterbacks are getting paid more than $50 million per season – they make a huge difference. As a team, you have to be able to complete passes. If you can't, they've reduced the game to you running the ball. If the opponent knows you can't complete passes, they'll take out your best running plays, you won't get across midfield, and the game will be over. When you can complete passes, you can play the total game of offense.

MOST VALUABLE PLAYER

As Coach Hagen alluded to in the Advanced Tactics section, quarterbacks are hugely valuable to their respective American football teams; whatever the level. And in the NFL, it is often quarterbacks who are named Most Valuable Players of seasons and Super Bowls. Here is an explanation of a term you will here quite a bit when on your NFL journey. This is the term given to the NFL's player of the season or the player of the game in the Super Bowl. The season-long Most Valuable Player is determined by a vote from a pool of 50 reporters. The award often goes to quarterbacks, with players from that position being named NFL MVP in each of the past 12 seasons. The reigning NFL MVP is Buffalo Bills quarterback Josh Allen.

The Super Bowl MVP is decided by a fan vote on NFL. com and also by votes from a 20-member media panel. Quarterbacks have been named Most Valuable Player in 34 of the 59 Super Bowls up to and including the 2024 NFL season, when Jalen Hurts, from the Philadelphia Eagles, was chosen.

The NFL Year

While the NFL action on the field runs from September to February, the league does a tremendous job of keeping American football at the forefront of everyone's minds all year round. There are significant events running throughout the calendar year, starting just a few short weeks after the NFL's newest champion has been crowned.

LATE FEBRUARY/EARLY MARCH . . . THE NFL COMBINE

The NFL Combine – held in Indianapolis each year due to the city's convenient travel links – signals the start of intense preparations for the next season, which doesn't actually kick off for another six months. As former Green Bay Packers and Dallas Cowboys head coach Mike McCarthy said: 'This is the starting line for our season.'

The NFL Combine is part track meet and part job fair as the 32 teams run a very extensive rule over more than 300 of the leading college football players who will enter that April's NFL Draft. Who gets an invite to the Combine is decided by the NFL's Player Selection Committee, which receives feedback from all 32 teams.

The Combine gives players a chance to present themselves and their skills to NFL scouts, general managers and head coaches. They are measured for everything from body fat and bone structure to the size of their hands and calves, put through a series of physical tests in the gym – including bench-pressing 225 pounds as many times as possible – and interviewed many times over.

Those interviews focus on the tactical elements of American football, but they also aim to unlock a player's psychological makeup. For example, quarterbacks are often asked questions to highlight their leadership skills or to expose their lack of them. . . 'You're on a bus travelling 100 miles per hour on a mountain road in Alaska. Where are you sitting?' Other teams will install basketball hoops into their meeting rooms to test a player's competitive nature.

Once they have been measured, given a full health check that includes heart and organ functions, and undergone those in-person interviews, the prospects will spend the next four days on the field. This work includes the 40-yard sprint, change-of-direction shuttle runs and other position-specific challenges.

While some players will have already cemented their status as top prospects for the NFL Draft because of their pedigree from playing well in college, it is fair to say that a good – or bad – performance in Indianapolis can completely transform the fortunes of many young athletes. Xavier Worthy ran the fastest 40-yard sprint in NFL Combine history in 2024 (4.21 seconds) and went from being an okay wide receiver to a first-round draft pick for the Chiefs.

MID-MARCH . . . NFL FREE AGENCY

The opening of the NFL's Free Agency signing period is a bit like the Premier League's Transfer Deadline Day, only in reverse. Teams come roaring out of the gate ready to spend some serious money (each club had a record $279.2 million to spend on its 53 players in 2025) during a key period for roster building ahead of the next season.

When NFL stars have played out their contracts (which typically range from one to five years in length), they become free agents and can hit the open market without any compensation being paid to their former team. A prominent example of this from another sport would be soccer star Kylian Mbappé's free transfer move from Paris Saint-Germain to Real Madrid in 2024.

While Free Agency results have been mixed since its introduction in 1993, three of the greatest quarterbacks in NFL history have been through the system with great success. Drew Brees spent the first five seasons of his career with the San Diego Chargers before joining the New Orleans Saints in 2006 and winning a Super Bowl in 2009. Peyton Manning starred for the Indianapolis Colts for 14 seasons before joining the Denver Broncos in 2012. He guided the AFC West club to a Super Bowl appearance in 2013 and to Super Bowl glory in 2015. And the greatest player of all, Tom Brady, moved to the Tampa Bay Buccaneers in 2020, immediately winning a Super Bowl with his new club after spending two decades with the New England Patriots.

Ahead of NFL Free Agency, each team can protect one out-of-contract player by placing the franchise tag on them. If the player has not agreed a long-term deal with his club by July, he is then bound to his existing team for another season and will be paid the average of the top five players at his position. A player can be tagged three times, but his price tag gets more expensive to his team with each passing year.

LATE APRIL . . . THE NFL DRAFT

Each April, the 32 teams select the leading college football players from across America to add to their rosters via the NFL Draft, which remains the league's flagship event of the offseason.

To create competitive balance, the worst team from the previous season picks first, the second-worst team picks second and so on, all the way up to the defending Super Bowl champions, who will pick last in the round. Rinse and repeat for seven rounds over three days. So, in theory, the very best players should go to the worst teams, although it never quite works out that way.

There can be a lot of jeopardy in the NFL Draft and players who were projected to be good or bad at the professional level can turn out to be the exact opposite. There have been some especially famous cases of unexpected hits and misses at the quarterback position. . .

— In 2000, every NFL team overlooked a skinny-looking quarterback out of Michigan multiple times. Six quarterbacks were chosen ahead of Tom Brady, who was finally picked by the New England Patriots in the sixth round (199th overall). While the 'Brady Six' disappeared with very few NFL highlights to their names, Brady became the greatest player who ever lived, winning seven Super Bowls.

— In 2017, the Chicago Bears chose North Carolina's Mitchell Trubisky with the second pick. Eight selections later, the Kansas City Chiefs rolled the dice on a promising but erratic quarterback by the name of Patrick Mahomes. Trubisky lasted just four seasons in Chicago and is now a reserve for the Buffalo Bills. Mahomes is the biggest challenger to Brady's status as the greatest of all time and had already won three Super Bowls by the age of 29.

— In 2021, the San Francisco 49ers traded three first-round picks (teams can wheel and deal their selections and future picks to move up and down draft boards) to select North Dakota State quarterback Trey Lance third overall. He started just four games in two seasons before being traded to the Dallas Cowboys, where he started just once in two years. He is now a backup for the Los Angeles Chargers.

— Fortunately for the 49ers, the 2022 NFL Draft saw them strike it lucky with the very last pick as they made Iowa State's Brock Purdy 'Mr Irrelevant', which is the nickname cruelly given to the final player selected each year. Purdy led the 49ers to the NFC Championship Game in his first NFL season and to the Super Bowl in his second, and has become one of the league's most productive quarterbacks.

NFL Network analyst and former scout Daniel Jeremiah said: 'Without question, the scariest moment for a scout is the morning of the first rookie minicamp (on-field practice sessions in early May). You've sold players and been in the room and lobbied for guys and you end up getting them and there is the euphoria when you pick them. You see it on TV when you watch the draft and everybody is high-fiving and hugging, thinking, "We've just got the best player ever." Nobody knows until you get out there on that field and I've seen the good and the bad.'

General managers are responsible for building their rosters via the NFL Draft, and Chicago's Ryan Poles explained how much work goes into preparing for those high-stakes days at the end of each April when he said: 'Our analytics team built me a draft simulator. In 2024, I probably did 115 drafts before I even got to the actual NFL Draft. And there's trades involved – there are a lot of different pop-up scenarios, there's the unexpected.

'There are really tough moments where you feel like you're one pick away from getting a player and they get snatched up right before. You know, you end up following their career to see how they do.'

As a live event and television show, the NFL Draft should not really work. The opening round features NFL Commissioner Roger Goodell on stage for more than four hours reading names off a card. That's it! And yet it rates higher than the playoffs for some of America's other leading sports and a record crowd of more than 775,000 fans attended the three-day event in Detroit in 2024.

Each year, the NFL Draft travels to a new city. Green Bay hosted the event in 2025, and the 2026 selection process will take place in Pittsburgh. Other cities to host the offseason extravaganza have included New York, Chicago, Philadelphia, Nashville, Kansas City and Las Vegas.

Wherever the NFL Draft is held, the calling of a player's name means the realisation of a childhood dream. That's why so many of the young men who are bear-hugged on stage by the NFL Commissioner find themselves in floods of tears.

Buffalo Bills quarterback Josh Allen, who was chosen in the first round in 2018, recalled: 'It was a very surreal feeling. I was thinking, "I was in junior college three years ago and now I'm here in the NFL." This is the only thing I've ever wanted to do since I was a little kid. I still get the chills thinking about it now.'

LATE-JULY TO MID-AUGUST . . . TRAINING CAMP

Each summer, NFL teams hold training camps to make their final preparations for the upcoming season and it is a time of great hope for players, coaches and fans who dream of Super Bowl glory. Tradition used to dictate that each team would go on the road to live and practise together for three to four weeks, often staying in dormitories normally reserved for college students. While most clubs now hold training camps at their own facilities, there are still some exceptions and 2024 saw seven teams – including the defending champions Kansas City Chiefs – venture further afield to get ready for the new season.

Given the brutally hot weather that spreads across America in late July and early August, players often refer to training camp as 'the dog days of summer'. They can certainly be long and challenging days on and off the field. Here is an example of an average day for a Baltimore Ravens player during training camp.

Baltimore Ravens Training Camp Day

6:00 – 9:00am	Breakfast	
6:30 – 7:30am	Treatment	
7:30 – 8:30am	Strength and Performance session	
8:45 – 9:45am	Practice 1	ACT (Walk-through of plays)
10:00 – 10:40am	Position Meetings	
10:45 – 12 noon	Team Meeting	
11:30 – 1:00pm	Lunch	
1:00 – 1:30pm	Specialised Performance Prep	
1:35 – 4:05pm	Practice 2	Practice and Conditioning (Mandatory weigh-in before and after practice)

4:10 – 4:40pm	Recovery/Restoration/Regeneration (Snack available)
5:00 – 6:30pm	Team Meeting/Offense and Defense Meetings
6:30 – 8:00pm	Dinner
6:30 – 8:00pm	Shuttle buses available to team hotel
10:30pm	Curfew/Bedtime

These vital practices are also a time of great intensity. Teams are not only running, throwing, blocking and tackling to get ready for the season, players are fighting for their jobs. Each club can carry 90 players in training camp – or 91 if they add an international athlete – but that number must be reduced to 53 for the regular season, which comes at the conclusion of training camp and three preseason games. The last thing a player wants to hear towards the end of training camp is: 'Coach wants to see you. And bring your playbook.' That means they are being cut from the team and their NFL dream could be over, although every cast-aside player still has that opportunity to be seen and signed by another club.

Without fear of gruelling schedules or the pressure of losing their job, fans have a much nicer time at training camps and see them as an absolute dream and a chance to see their favourite players up close and personal. Many sessions are open to the public in their entirety. The summer preparations carried out across the NFL are hardly shrouded in secrecy, but they are vital. Through the month of August – and often while still in training camp mode – each team will play three friendlies, known as exhibition or preseason games. While many veteran stars are held out of these games to make sure they are fit and ready for the September kick-off, these contests are crucial for those whose selection for the final roster is in the balance.

EARLY SEPTEMBER . . . OPENING WEEKEND

While the NFL gives us plenty to talk about all year, the reality is that the offseason can be a long one when it comes to on-field action. If a team fails to make the playoffs in their previous campaign, that season will end in early January, meaning there is an eight-month wait before meaningful games can be played again. Even a successful team that makes a championship run has a long seven-month wait from early February to the beginning of September.

That can leave players and fans starving for an NFL feast come the first week of the new season, which traditionally begins at the home of the reigning Super Bowl champions on a Thursday night.

The Kansas City Chiefs hosted the 2023 and 2024 season-openers, and safety Justin Reid said: 'It's crazy. The energy is just electric and it travels down to us on the field. When you have that noise at your back and they're supporting you, it's an incredible feeling.'

The excitement is not just born out of emotional players feeding off hyped-up fans. Opening weekend brings a freshness, as Baltimore Ravens quarterback Lamar Jackson – the NFL's Most Valuable Player in 2018 and 2023 – explained: 'You've been going weeks and weeks against your own teammates like they're your opponents and then you finally get to go against somebody else you haven't been seeing each and every day for the past two months. Then it's time to let the chips fly!'

The majority of NFL opening weekend games are played on the Sunday, although the 2024 and 2025 season curtain-raisers also featured on Friday and Monday. And it doesn't matter if you're a fresh-faced rookie or a greybeard veteran, the first game of any season is special.

Future Hall of Fame quarterback Aaron Rodgers, who has played 20 NFL seasons, said: 'When I take the field for the first time and they announce, "at quarterback, Aaron Rodgers", it still gives me chills right now to think about that ovation.'

SEPTEMBER TO NOVEMBER . . . INTERNATIONAL GAMES

The NFL has been playing regular season games internationally since the 2006 season. And while the league's global adventure began in Mexico with the San Francisco

49ers defeating the Arizona Cardinals, the greatest successes have been enjoyed further afield.

Since 2007, London, England, has played host to regular season games in every year except for a Covid-19-impacted 2020 campaign. By the end of the 2025 season, a total of 42 regular season games will have been played in London, featuring all 32 NFL teams at least once. Baltimore Ravens quarterback Lamar Jackson is among the many stars to have enjoyed the experience. The two-time NFL Most Valuable Player led his team to victory at Tottenham Hotspur Stadium in 2023 and said: 'It was phenomenal. The atmosphere was crazy.'

Germany joined the NFL's international party in 2022 as the great Tom Brady led the Tampa Bay Buccaneers to victory over the Seattle Seahawks in Munich's Allianz Arena. After that contest, Brady said it was 'one of the greatest football experiences' he had enjoyed, and added: 'Everyone who was a part of that experience got to have a pretty amazing memory for the rest of their lives.'

The NFL has played four games in Germany thus far, spread across Munich and Frankfurt, and unveiled Berlin as a new host city in 2025. In 2024, the NFL played its first regular season game in Sao Paolo, Brazil, as the Philadelphia Eagles were victorious against the Green Bay Packers. And in 2025, the league debuts in Dublin, Ireland, and Madrid, Spain. Those two contests brought the total of regular season games played across Europe in 2025 to six.

NFL Commissioner Roger Goodell expects rapid expansion of the NFL's international games in the future, as he explained: 'I think the logical step for us is that if we expand our season from the 17 regular season games to 18 regular season games, reduce our preseason from three to two games. I can see us, at the same time saying, "You know, everyone's going to play an international game every year." So, we'd have 16 international regular season games in every season. Not on the same weekend, of course, but throughout the season. And I think that's something for us to shoot for in the next several years. I think the clubs are prepared to do that.

'I think, if we go back to that Formula One thought process, we see how they move races around and how that electrifies each one of those communities. I think we can do that by taking our game and sharing it with those fans.

'This is a unique time in our history to advance our growth, particularly internationally. It may be the single-most important growth moment in our history.'

LATE NOVEMBER . . . THANKSGIVING DAY

America's annual Thanksgiving Day holiday falls on the fourth Thursday of November. It's a time for food, family and football, because NFL games have become as much a part of the celebrations as turkey, stuffing and pumpkin pie.

NFL games have been a yearly tradition on Thanksgiving since 1934, when Detroit Lions owner George A. Richards set up a game against the Chicago Bears to boost flagging attendances. Chicago won 19-16, but the Lions were winners at the gate, as a sell-out crowd of 26,000 witnessed the historic contest.

The NFL wanted to add a regular team to the late-afternoon slot in the 1960s, but few teams were interested at the time, as they worried the television ratings would not be strong. But Cowboys general manager Tex Schramm believed any publicity would be good for a team struggling for recognition, so the Cowboys began playing on Thanksgiving in 1966. Dallas enjoyed success on and off the field, growing massively to become known as 'America's Team'.

In every season since 1978, the Lions have played in the early slot, kicking off at 12.30pm US east coast time (5.30pm in the UK), with the Cowboys playing at 4.30pm (9.30pm). In 2006, the NFL added a night game, which features other teams from around the league. And in 2023, there was a new twist to the holiday weekend as the NFL played on Black Friday for the first time, with the Miami Dolphins recording a 34-13 win over the New York Jets.

There have been some incredible individual performances on Thanksgiving Day, including Dallas quarterback Troy Aikman throwing for 455 yards against the Minnesota

Vikings in 1998 or Peyton Manning, of the Indianapolis Colts, throwing six touchdown passes against Detroit in 2004. But Thanksgiving has also served up some of the weirdest headlines in NFL history. Here is a brief look at a few of those unforgettable moments.

Leon Lett slides into infamy

The 1993 meeting between the Miami Dolphins and the Dallas Cowboys already had a special feel to it as a rare November storm in Texas covered the field in a blanket of snow and ice. The defending Super Bowl-champion Cowboys led the playoff-chasing Dolphins 14-13 as Miami lined up for a difficult 41-yard field goal attempt with 15 seconds remaining. Pete Stoyanovich's kick was blocked by Jimmie Jones. Game over? Not quite. The ball rolled towards the Dallas end zone, and it would be declared dead as soon as it stopped moving, giving the Cowboys the victory. But defensive lineman Leon Lett – who made a massive blunder in the previous season's Super Bowl by celebrating a touchdown too soon and having the ball knocked from his grasp – slid in to recover a ball that didn't need to be recovered. He kicked the ball to the one-yard line, where Miami recovered. Stoyanovich then slotted an easy 19-yard field goal and Miami escaped with a 16-14 win.

The Butt Fumble

The New England Patriots' 49-19 victory over the New York Jets in 2012 was so one-sided that it was largely forgettable. But there was one moment that will live forever in NFL history, even if the Jets and their quarterback at the time, Mark Sanchez, would rather we forget all about 'The Butt Fumble'. The Jets were trailing 14-0 in the second quarter when Sanchez took the snap from the center and turned the wrong way, meaning he had missed the chance to hand the ball to his running back. Sanchez tried to make amends by running the ball himself. But he sprinted into the backside of offensive lineman Brandon

Moore, fumbling the ball for New England's Steve Gregory
to score on a 32-yard touchdown. Sanchez recalled: 'It's
embarrassing. You screw up the play and I'm trying to do the
right thing. I slide in the worst spot I possibly could – right into
Brandon Moore. That sucked.' Jets head coach Rex Ryan was
hardly supportive of his quarterback after the game, as he
remarked: 'You always teach a quarterback, "Don't make a bad
play worse." Well, we made it worse. I don't know what Sanchez
was doing. It was just a disaster.'

Heads or tails?

The Pittsburgh Steelers and Detroit Lions were tied 16-16
at the end of their Thanksgiving Day game in 1998. So,
they headed into sudden-death overtime. Steelers running
back Jerome Bettis appeared to call 'tails' and, with the
coin landing on tails, that would have given Pittsburgh first
chance to win the game. But referee Phil Luckett announced
on the field: 'He said heads, it is a tails.' Luckett ruled that
Bettis said heads and then changed to tails with the coin in
mid-air, giving the football to the Lions. Detroit took that
first possession down the field to set up Jason Hanson's
42-yard field goal that secured a controversial 19-16 victory. Steelers defensive back Carnell Lake, who was at
midfield for the coin toss, as one of Pittsburgh's captains,
recalled: 'I was so shocked. I was ready to have a full-out protest
right there on the field. Sit down and lay on the 50-yard line until
the police drug us off.' The controversy led to a rule change,
which meant calls could no longer be made with the coin
in mid-air.

Out of the way, coach!

The Pittsburgh Steelers had just cut the Baltimore Ravens'
second-half lead to 13-7 on Thanksgiving Day in 2013 when
they kicked off to their division rivals. Baltimore's Jacoby
Jones fielded the ball at his goal-line and was on his way to
a key touchdown as he covered 73 yards down the sideline
before turning slightly back in-field, where he was tackled

by Cortez Allen. The reason for the diversion? Jones was forced to avoid Steelers head coach Mike Tomlin, who was standing slightly in the field of play with his back to the action watching the return on the big screen. Ravens fans were further infuriated by the sight of Tomlin giggling moments after the play. Reflecting on the infamous incident years later, Tomlin said: **'It's just one of those unfortunate moments of life. I was watching the JumboTron and lost track of where I was. Such is life.'** Baltimore didn't score a touchdown on that drive, but they did make Tomlin's 'interference' easier to swallow as they battled to a 22-20 victory.

No shoe, no problem!

In a 2010 meeting with the Cincinnati Bengals, New York Jets kick-returner Brad Smith ran so fast on an 89-yard touchdown that he sprinted all the way out of his shoe. The Jets were leading 17-10 in the fourth quarter when Smith caught the ball at his own 11-yard line and weaved through would-be tacklers from the Bengals. At midfield, as he reached top speed, Smith's left shoe flew off, leaving New York's explosive star to cover the final 50 yards with only one boot! It was a key play in the Jets' 26-10 victory. After the game, Smith joked: **'All that running in the back yard when I was little with no shoes on with my brother. I think that helped.'**

JANUARY . . . THE PLAYOFFS

At the end of the NFL's regular season, 14 teams remain on the road to the Super Bowl and the intensity levels rise significantly as 18 weeks of league play are followed by the ultimate cup competition and a straight knockout tournament. Win and you advance along the road to the Super Bowl, lose and you have eight long and difficult months to think about where it all went wrong.

The playoffs feature an AFC and an NFC tournament, with each conference providing a champion to meet in the Super Bowl. Seven teams qualify from each conference – the four division champions and the three clubs with the next-best record, known as wild cards. The top seed in each conference receives an automatic bye to the second round. There are three playoff rounds before the Super Bowl . . . the Wild Card Round, Divisional Round (Super Bowl quarter-finals) and the Conference Championships (Super Bowl semi-finals). In each round, the highest seed plays the lowest seed. For example, in the Wild Card Round, the AFC's second seed will play the seventh-ranked team, six will play three and five will play four. The same pattern is repeated in the NFC. When the top seed enters the fray, they will play at home so long as they remain in the playoffs and always face the lowest-remaining seed.

Given the high stakes, some of the NFL's most famous plays have occurred during the playoffs: Pittsburgh's 'Immaculate Reception', the 'Minneapolis Miracle' and 'The Catch', featuring Joe Montana and Dwight Clark of the San Francisco 49ers, are just a few you can read about in this book. Those and many more like them are a reminder that big plays – good and bad – that happen in the playoffs can forever write the names of players and coaches into the NFL history books.

FEBRUARY . . . THE SUPER BOWL

America comes to a standstill every February to watch a new champion of the NFL be crowned in the Super Bowl. It has often been reported that Super Bowl Sunday sees a significant drop in crime rates across the USA and is also the slowest weekend of the year for weddings.

Despite offering up the very best of Americana and sporting glitz and glamour, the Super Bowl is no longer limited to the United States. In fact, the Super Bowl has been broadcast live on British television every year since Washington defeated Miami at the end of the 1982 season. It has become a global phenomenon, with 2024's game between the Kansas City Chiefs and San Francisco 49ers watched by more than 62.5 million fans around the world and official NFL watch parties being held in Australia,

Brazil, France, Germany, Ghana, Mexico and the United Kingdom.

The Super Bowl first made a humble entry onto the American sports scene at the end of the 1966 season and was known as the AFL-NFL Championship Game. It did not officially become the Super Bowl until the third title showdown, between the New York Jets and Baltimore Colts, in the 1969 season. The name was the brainchild of Kansas City Chiefs owner Lamar Hunt, who wanted to make the title game seem grander and had been watching his children play with a popular toy called the 'Super Ball'.

With just one trophy up for grabs in each NFL season, to play in a Super Bowl is huge, as defensive tackle Ndamukong Suh, who played in the big game three times with the Los Angeles Rams, Tampa Bay Buccaneers and Philadelphia Eagles, explained: **'The Super Bowl is one of those great games to be able to play in. It's amazing. Nothing else matters – you have to go out there and win it.'**

Linebacker Ray Lewis won two Super Bowls with the Baltimore Ravens in a Hall of Fame career. His first came in Super Bowl 35 at the end of the 2000 season – his fifth in the NFL. And his second success came in Super Bowl 47, during the 2012 campaign – his final game as an NFL superstar.

Lewis recalled: **'There is no greater feeling than touching confetti for the first time as a Super Bowl champion. And the second time I won came at the end of a game where I strapped on the cleats for the last time. I was able to leave on my terms.'**

The Super Bowl has become much more than an American football game. Each contest is preceded by a week of media engagements and showbiz parties. And Super Bowl Sunday offers something for everyone, with sports fans tuning in for the game, while others like to watch halftime shows that have featured a who's who of global stars, from Madonna to Beyoncé and Lady Gaga, to Michael Jackson, Prince, U2 and Bruce Springsteen. Then there are the American television adverts, which are an entertainment proposition in their own right. And they have to be good when you consider that companies were paying FOX up to

$8 million for an advertising spot in their coverage of Super Bowl 59 at the end of the 2024 season.

The Super Bowl has served up some iconic and historic moments. Here, in chronological order, are some of the best games played in recent times.

Super Bowl 23 (1988 season)
San Francisco 49ers 20-16 Cincinnati Bengals

The 49ers were heavy favourites to win a third Super Bowl but found themselves trailing Cincinnati 16-13 with just over three minutes remaining. San Francisco quarterback Joe Montana drove his team 92 yards to glory. Along the way he lived up to his 'Joe Cool' nickname by pointing out John Candy in the crowd to teammates during a TV time-out. Montana threw the game-winning 10-yard touchdown pass to John Taylor with 34 seconds remaining and said: **'Throwing a touchdown pass to win the Super Bowl on your last drive of the game is something I did a thousand times before in the back yard with my best friend at receiver. As a quarterback, it's a dream come true to win any game that way, but especially a Super Bowl.'**

Super Bowl 25 (1990 season)
New York Giants 20-19 Buffalo Bills

The Giants – led by an assistant coach who would go on to historic greatness in Bill Belichick – produced a masterful defensive display to neuter one of the most high-powered attacks in the NFL. With assistance from backup quarter-back Jeff Hostetler, New York fought and scrapped their way to a one-point lead with just seconds to play. Buffalo's Scott Norwood had a chance to win the game with a 47-yard field goal, but he sent his kick wide right and is forever associated with that moment in an otherwise successful career. It was the first of four straight Super Bowl defeats for the Bills.

Super Bowl 34 (1999 season)
St. Louis Rams 23-16 Tennessee Titans

This roller-coaster of a game provided the fairytale moment for Rams quarterback Kurt Warner, who had previously been out of American football and working as a supermarket shelf stacker before grabbing what was his final opportunity in St. Louis. Warner and the Rams opened up a 16-0 lead, but the Titans fought back and tied the game with just over two minutes remaining. Warner quickly struck on a 73-yard touchdown pass to Isaac Bruce to give the Rams a seven-point lead with 1:54 left. Titans quarterback Steve McNair moved his team into scoring range but, on the final play of the game, he completed a pass to Kevin Dyson only to see his receiver tackled one yard short of the end zone by Rams linebacker Mike Jones.

Super Bowl 36 (2001 season)
New England Patriots 20-17 St. Louis Rams

Emotions were running high at the Superdome in New Orleans for the first Super Bowl played after the 9/11 attacks on America. The contest was expected to result in Kurt Warner and the Rams being crowned champions for a second time. But it marked a first Super Bowl success for the Patriots and fresh-faced quarterback Tom Brady. The real hero of the hour, though, was New England's Adam Vinatieri, who kicked the game-winning 48-yard field goal as time expired to give his team a 20-17 victory. After making the first of three game-winners in Super Bowls, Vinatieri said: **'As a young boy, I dreamed of being able to play in a Super Bowl and to win it as the kicker and have the game come down to the last play is the ultimate. There's no better feeling outside the birth of my children.'**

Super Bowl 42 (2007 season)
New York Giants 17-14 New England Patriots

The Patriots were strongly favoured to record just the second perfect season in NFL history as they took on a

Giants team that won just nine games before finding their form during the NFC playoffs. New England appeared to have secured their place in NFL history when Randy Moss scored on a touchdown pass from Tom Brady with 2:42 remaining. But the Giants produced one of the most remarkable plays in NFL history as Eli Manning completed a 32-yard pass to David Tyree, who pinned the ball against his head in what would become known as 'The Helmet Catch'. Moments later, Manning threw a touchdown pass to Plaxico Burress and the Giants were the unlikeliest of Super Bowl champions.

Super Bowl 43 (2008 season)
Pittsburgh Steelers 27-23 Arizona Cardinals

Led by that season's NFL Most Valuable Player in quarterback Kurt Warner – previously of the Rams – the Arizona Cardinals took this thrilling Super Bowl down to the wire. Arizona – who had won just nine games during the regular season – moved into a dramatic and unexpected 23-20 lead with 2:37 remaining as Warner connected on a 64-yard touchdown pass with Larry Fitzgerald. But Ben Roethlisberger delivered late heroics for the Steelers as he threw an inch-perfect winning touchdown strike to Santonio Holmes with 35 seconds remaining. Roethlisberger said: **'That's every kid's dream. You're aware of the magnitude of the occasion but you're not thinking about this being the biggest moment of your career – you're just trying to play. That last throw to Santonio was a blur at the time but, looking back on it, that was a great memory.'** The win meant the Steelers became the first team to win six Super Bowls.

Super Bowl 49 (2014 season)
New England Patriots 28-24 Seattle Seahawks

This monumental clash in the Arizona desert pitted a powerful New England attack led by Tom Brady against one of the best defenses of its generation in the Seattle

Seahawks, who were the NFL's defending champions. Yet it was a thrilling contest decided by New England's defense and Seattle's attack. The Patriots led 28-24 following Brady's fourth touchdown pass of the evening, but the Seahawks seemed set to steal the Vince Lombardi Trophy at the death. But on second down from the New England one-yard line with 26 seconds remaining, Seattle opted for a risky Russell Wilson throw instead of handing the ball to one of the league's best and most powerful running backs in Marshawn Lynch. And disaster struck as Wilson was intercepted by little-known defensive back Malcolm Butler at the goal-line, clinching a fourth Super Bowl win for Brady and the Patriots in the most stunning fashion. Butler recalled: **'If I was (Seahawks head coach) Pete Carroll, I'm running that football. But that was a nice play call . . . I loved it! I said to myself, "If they throw the ball, it's on." The ball was coming so fast. I had to treat it like a baby and catch it soft. I most definitely knew I had done something special.'**

Super Bowl 51 (2016 season)
New England Patriots 34-28 Atlanta Falcons

The Patriots won the first Super Bowl to go into overtime after completing a memorable comeback against the Atlanta Falcons. Atlanta led 28-3 midway through the third quarter, but Tom Brady would not be denied as he threw two late touchdown passes and a two-point conversion to take the game to sudden death. And on the first drive of overtime, New England won the contest on James White's two-yard run. Former Patriots general manager Scott Pioli was working for the Falcons at that time and warned against celebrating too early, as he recalled: **'People kept patting me on the back and I whipped around and said, "You people don't get it. That number 12 across the field is Freddy Kruger. He's coming back and he's gonna get a bunch of us. I just hope he doesn't get us all." '** Brady did and the Patriots were champions once more.

CHAPTER 06

Super Bowl 52 (2017 season)
Philadelphia Eagles 41-33 New England Patriots

Led by backup quarterback Nick Foles, the Philadelphia Eagles won a dramatic Super Bowl that saw both teams combine for a record 1,151 offensive yards and just one punt. Foles threw for 373 yards and three touchdowns, including the go-ahead score to tight end Zach Ertz midway through the final period. Foles had earlier scored on a touchdown catch of his own on a play known as 'The Philly Special'. When Brandon Graham sacked Tom Brady and forced a late fumble, the Eagles added a Jake Elliott field goal with 1:04 remaining to complete the scoring. Despite that lost fumble, Brady was excellent even in pursuit of a losing cause as he threw for 505 yards and three touchdowns.

Super Bowl 57 (2022 season)
Kansas City Chiefs 38-35 Philadelphia Eagles

After an incredible back-and-forth duel between Kansas City's Patrick Mahomes and Philadelphia's Jalen Hurts – the first Black quarterbacks to face off against each other in a Super Bowl – it was the Chiefs who emerged with a third NFL crown after Harrison Butker kicked a game-winning 27-yard field goal with eight seconds remaining. The Eagles looked to be in control at halftime as they led 24-14, and Mahomes had re-injured the ankle that had caused him great pain during the playoffs. But in winning his second Super Bowl, Mahomes was at his brilliant best in the second half and was named the game's Most Valuable Player. Reflecting on that huge win, Mahomes said: **'I enjoy playing in those big games. Winning them is obviously better than losing them but just to be a part of them is something special.'**

CHAPTER 07

The NFL Timeline

1920

On 17 September 1920, a group of men gathered in Canton, Ohio, at the Hupmobile showroom of Ralph Hay, who also owned the hometown Bulldogs. The result of the meeting was the birth of the National Football League.

1921

The Akron Pros were voted champions of the NFL's inaugural 1920 season, but not until 30 April 1921. League titles were based on regular season records in the early years and were often hotly disputed due to teams playing different numbers of games against differing standards of opponents.

1933

The NFL's first official championship game was played in 1933, with the Chicago Bears recording a 23-21 victory over the New York Giants.

1936

The NFL Draft was held for the first time at the Ritz-Carlton Hotel in Philadelphia. The hometown Eagles had the first pick and chose running back Jay Berwanger from the University of Chicago.

1940

The NFL Championship Game was broadcast on national radio for the first time, reaching 120 stations via the Mutual Broadcasting System. The Chicago Bears beat Washington 73-0 in what is still the most one-sided game in NFL history.

1951

The NFL Championship Game was televised coast to coast for the first time on The DuMont Network. The Los Angeles Rams defeated the Cleveland Browns 24-17.

1960

The rival American Football League – formed by Dallas Texans owner Lamar Hunt, whose family still owns the franchise now known as the Kansas City Chiefs – began play with eight teams. The Houston Oilers were crowned as the inaugural champions.

1967

The first Super Bowl – which capped the 1966 season – pitted the NFL champion Green Bay Packers against the AFL champion Kansas City Chiefs in Los Angeles. The Packers ran out the convincing 35-10 winners.

1970

The NFL merged with the American Football League, which had risen to 10 teams by the 1969 season. Bringing the AFL teams into the fold took the total of NFL clubs from 16 to 26.

1972

The Miami Dolphins became the first – and still only – undefeated team in NFL history, capping a season of 17 wins and no losses with a 14-7 victory over Washington in Super Bowl 7.

1983

Super Bowl 17 – which was played on 30 January 1983, to conclude the 1982 season – was the first to be televised live on British television on Channel 4. Washington beat the Miami Dolphins 27-17.

2006 The Arizona Cardinals defeated the San Francisco 49ers 31-14 in the first regular season NFL game to be played outside of the United States. The contest drew a record 103,467 fans to Mexico City's Azteca Stadium.

2007 In the first NFL regular season game to be played outside of North America, the New York Giants recorded a 13-10 win over the Miami Dolphins at London's Wembley Stadium.

2019 The NFL celebrated its 100th season. The Kansas City Chiefs were crowned champions after a 31-20 win over the San Francisco 49ers in Super Bowl 54.

2025 The Philadelphia Eagles were crowned champions of the NFL's 2024 campaign with a comprehensive 40-22 victory over the Kansas City Chiefs in Super Bowl 59, which was played in the Superdome in New Orleans on 9 February 2025.

The American Football Conference (AFC)

The American Football Conference is largely made up of teams who played in the American Football League before the 1970 merger with the NFL. The Buffalo Bills, Cincinnati Bengals, Denver Broncos, Kansas City Chiefs, Las Vegas Raiders, Los Angeles Chargers, Miami Dolphins, New England Patriots, New York Jets and Tennessee Titans can all trace their roots back to the old AFL.

Of the 16 teams playing in four divisions across the AFC, two franchises have dominated in recent times. In the past 24 seasons, from 2001 to 2024, the Patriots and Chiefs have represented the conference in the Super Bowl 14 times, winning nine Vince Lombardi Trophies between them during that span.

The AFC is also home to arguably the four best quarterbacks in the NFL in Buffalo's Josh Allen (the 2025 reigning NFL Most Valuable Player), Baltimore's two-time NFL MVP Lamar Jackson, Cincinnati's league-leading passer from 2024 in Joe Burrow and three-time Super Bowl champion Patrick Mahomes, of the Kansas City Chiefs.

With another group of excellent quarterbacks nipping at the heels of that quartet in the form of Justin Herbert (Los Angeles Chargers), C.J. Stroud (Houston Texans) and Tua Tagovailoa (Miami Dolphins), the action is always intense in the AFC.

BALTIMORE RAVENS

FIRST SEASON
1996

OWNER
Steve Bisciotti

DIVISION
AFC North

HEAD COACH
John Harbaugh

COLOURS
**Purple,
black and
metallic gold**

STADIUM
**M&T Bank
Stadium
(70,745)**

NFL TITLES/SUPER BOWLS
2 (2000, 2012)

BALTIMORE RAVENS

INTRODUCING THE RAVENS . . .

The Ravens took flight in 1996 when then-owner Art Modell took his Cleveland Browns and relocated them to Baltimore. The NFL wanted the Browns' nickname and records to remain in Cleveland (that club returned to the league in 1999), so Baltimore's new team was named the Ravens after former resident Edgar Allen Poe's 'The Raven' poem.

The Ravens have been perennially competitive. They enjoyed early success as their first NFL Draft netted a pair of Hall of Fame stars in offensive tackle Jonathan Ogden and linebacker Ray Lewis. That cornerstone pair was instrumental in Baltimore's first league title, which came with a 34-7 win over the New York Giants in Super Bowl 35 at the end of the 2000 season.

Baltimore picked up a second league crown in defeating the San Francisco 49ers 34-31 in Super Bowl 47. Their two championship teams were built 12 years apart, boasted different head coaches (Brian Billick for the first and John Harbaugh for the second) and quarterbacks, but displayed many of the same traits. Ravens teams have long been built on physicality, toughness and iron-clad discipline.

Today's version of the Ravens – led by two-time NFL Most Valuable Player Lamar Jackson at quarterback – remains a regular contender and one of the most physical teams in the league. Explosive stars like Jackson and running back Derrick Henry have seen the Ravens add offensive firepower to their defensive muscle and Baltimore have reached the playoffs five times since 2019. Given their winning culture, the Ravens are likely to remain in the Super Bowl conversation for quite some time.

HOME

M&T BANK STADIUM

The Ravens have called M&T Bank Stadium home since 1998 and they've been playing a pretty successful tune on what was once the site of a piano-making factory. The five-level, 70,745-seat venue turns purple on gamedays as passionate Ravens fans cheer on their team. The stadium could be familiar to some Premier League fans, as the likes of Tottenham, Liverpool, Manchester City, Arsenal and Chelsea have played preseason games there while touring the USA.

HEAD COACH

JOHN HARBAUGH

The Ravens are led by 62-year-old John Harbaugh, who is now in his 17th season in Baltimore, making him one of the NFL's longest-serving coaches. During his first 17 years, Harbaugh led the Ravens to the playoffs 12 times, as well as six division titles and a Super Bowl win. A proven winner, Harbaugh has balanced being tough and adaptable, as he explains: 'Principles are written in stone, but methods are drawn in the dirt. We can change the methods and the way we do things, but our eternal principles remain the same – hard work, discipline, attention to detail and teamwork.'

LAMAR JACKSON – QUARTERBACK

Baltimore's biggest star, quarterback Lamar Jackson, is one of the most electrifying weapons the NFL has ever seen. When you think of a quarterback, your first thought is likely to be of a player firing accurate passes downfield. Jackson – who has been named the league's Most Valuable Player in 2019 and 2023 – can definitely do that. But his true worth to the Ravens comes in his versatility and in his sheer explosive athleticism. Jackson is the best running quarterback in NFL history and he is the only player at his position to twice top 1,000 rushing yards in a single season – a milestone normally reserved for leading running backs. Now in his eighth season, the four-time all-star is an evolving weapon. The 28-year-old still drives defenses mad with his speed and elusiveness, but Jackson now uses that ability to avoid tackles for multiple reasons – to set off on a run downfield or to buy time before throwing to a wide-open receiver. Jackson admits: 'I absolutely enjoy being able to play with that kind of freedom.' In 2024, Jackson posted a passer rating of 119.6 – the fourth-best single-season effort in NFL history. He was named the NFL's first-team All-Pro (best of the best) quarterback. With plenty of plaudits and honours already in his locker, Jackson's remaining goal will be to lead Baltimore to Super Bowl glory.

RAY LEWIS – LINEBACKER

The driving force during Baltimore's Super Bowl wins was linebacker Ray Lewis, who was one of the most ferocious tacklers and best leaders in NFL history. The 13-time all-star made more than 2,000 tackles while spending his entire 17-year career with the Ravens. In Baltimore's first Super Bowl win, Lewis was named the game's Most Valuable Player, as he led a dominant defense against the New York Giants. His second Super Bowl title came in his final season and saw Lewis on the field fending off a late San Francisco 49ers comeback. In between those successes, Lewis wreaked havoc on ball-carriers across the league. He boasted great instincts, was fast and could hit like a runaway train. But Lewis believes the reason for his greatness was simple, as he reveals: 'I was never the biggest, I was never the fastest and I was never the strongest – but I've never met a man who will out-work me. I chase pain. Most people run away from that pain. Work ethic is the number one thing you need to succeed in life.' Lewis was inducted into the Pro Football Hall of Fame in 2018 and named in the NFL's 100th Anniversary team in 2019.

MOMENT IN TIME

THE NIGHT THE LIGHTS WENT OUT!

Baltimore's second title win, which came against San Francisco in the 2012 season, was one of the league's most unique championship showdowns. Super Bowl 47 – played in New Orleans – saw the Ravens make a strong start, opening a 21-6 lead through three Joe Flacco touchdown passes. The Niners were in further trouble when Baltimore's Jacoby Jones fielded the opening kick-off of the second half and returned it 108 yards for a touchdown, giving the Ravens a commanding 28-6 lead. The 49ers needed a miracle. What they got was one of the most famous power cuts in sporting history. With 13:22 left in the third quarter, the lights went out, plunging the Superdome into an eerie semi-darkness. The power was down for 34 surreal minutes and, when the lights came back on, momentum shifted and what threatened to be a one-sided Super Bowl became a classic. San Francisco scored the game's next three touchdowns. The Ravens were clinging to a late 34-29 lead, but the 49ers had the ball at Baltimore's seven-yard line with a chance to steal the game inside the final two minutes. Baltimore's defense dug deep and held, crowning the Ravens as winners of a Super Bowl that will never be forgotten.

★ **DID YOU KNOW?** ★

Super Bowl 47, which saw the Ravens defeat the 49ers during the 2012 season, was the first to pit head coaching brothers against each other in the NFL's big game. John Harbaugh led Baltimore against his younger sibling and former NFL quarterback, Jim, then head coach of San Francisco.

BUFFALO BILLS

FIRST SEASON
1960

DIVISION
AFC East

COLOURS
Royal blue, red, white and navy blue

OWNER
Terry and Kim Pegula

HEAD COACH
Sean McDermott

STADIUM
Highmark Stadium (71,608)

NFL TITLES/SUPER BOWLS:
0

BUFFALO BILLS

INTRODUCING THE BILLS . . .

Throughout a history that has ticked into a 65th season, the Buffalo Bills have played some exciting American football and have been very competitive. But that has yet to result in Super Bowl glory and the Bills remain one of 12 teams never to lift the Vince Lombardi Trophy.

They have come close, though. In four straight seasons, from 1990 to 1993, Buffalo fielded one of the greatest teams in league history under Hall of Fame head coach Marv Levy, brilliant quarterback Jim Kelly and a collection of massive stars. The results were historic and frustrating – the Bills are the only team in NFL history to lose four consecutive Super Bowls.

That heartbreak hit hard. Buffalo recorded a playoff win against the Miami Dolphins at the end of the 1995 season, but their next knockout victory did not come until a quarter of a century later in the 2020 campaign. A period of 17 years without a playoff appearance saw Buffalo roll through nine head coaches.

Their current challenge is driven by superstar quarterback Josh Allen, who is one of the NFL's most exciting athletes and the league's reigning Most Valuable Player, having won that award in the 2024 season. Few are as valuable to their NFL team as Allen is to the Bills – and he is beloved by one of the most passionate fan bases in America.

But Buffalo have still not found Super Bowl joy, thanks to a familiar foe. They have won five straight AFC East crowns but have been knocked out of the playoffs four times since 2020 by the Patrick Mahomes-led Kansas City Chiefs.

HIGHMARK STADIUM

The Bills have been playing at Highmark Stadium since 1973, upgrading one of the NFL's older and colder venues in 1998 and 2013. Given the wintry elements that can affect contests in Buffalo, the 71,608-seat stadium has witnessed games with challenging weather, especially when the snow rolls in off Lake Erie. The Bills are building a 62,000-seat open-air stadium just across the street. The $1.4 billion venue is scheduled to open in 2026.

SEAN McDERMOTT

The Bills are led by 51-year-old Sean McDermott, who has massively improved the fortunes of the team during his time in charge. In 2017, the former Carolina Panthers defensive coordinator guided Buffalo to their first playoff appearance since 1999 and, in 2020, he oversaw the team's first visit to the AFC Championship Game (the Super Bowl semi-finals) since 1993. The former college safety has taken the Bills to the playoffs in seven of his first eight seasons in Buffalo.

JOSH ALLEN – QUARTERBACK

Buffalo's driving force is quarterback Josh Allen and he is an absolute force of nature who gives his all every single weekend. Allen plays with a reckless abandon that makes him hard to predict and even harder to defend. His success has been clear for all to see and, after growing up on a cotton farm in the small California town of Firebaugh, Allen is now one of America's biggest sports stars. One of the joys of the NFL is to watch the all-star quarterback on top form. Allen can do it all, as he proved when leading the NFL with 51 total touchdowns in 2023 (33 passing and 18 rushing, including the playoffs). He backed that up with 47 total touchdowns in 2024. Allen boasts arguably the league's strongest arm, which means no area of the field is safe from his powerful throws. And he is a devastating runner who can race away from defenders, although this fearless leader is just as likely to pile through or hurdle over would-be tacklers. At 29 and only in his eighth season, there is plenty of time for Allen to deliver a long-awaited Super Bowl trophy to Buffalo. Asked if he dreams of such a moment, the $55 million-per-year quarterback replied: 'Every night. I can only picture so much because I know for a fact that it's going to be better than what is in my mind.' Few would begrudge Allen his moment in the ultimate NFL spotlight.

BRUCE SMITH – DEFENSIVE END

Buffalo's Super Bowl teams of the early 1990s featured great Hall of Famers in quarterback Jim Kelly, wide receivers Andre Reed and James Lofton, and running back Thurman Thomas. Their dominant leader on the other side was defensive end Bruce Smith, who is hailed as one of the greatest defenders in NFL history. First choice in the 1985 NFL Draft, Smith easily surpassed lofty expectations. Playing from 1985 to 2003, Smith's 200 career sacks are an NFL record that still stands today. With an unblockable mix of power and speed, Smith made life hell for NFL quarterbacks. And Smith was as consistent as he was great, recording at least 10 sacks in 13 of his 19 seasons (another NFL record) and was twice named NFL Defensive Player of the Year. Like Buffalo's offensive stars, Smith is a member of the Pro Football Hall of Fame.

THE COMEBACK

During Buffalo's Super Bowl years, coach Marv Levy regularly praised the 'intestinal fortitude' of his team as they bounced back from annual disappointment. Levy's Bills severely tested that mental strength as they hosted the Houston Oilers in the first round of the 1992 season's playoffs. With star quarterback Jim Kelly sidelined through injury, backup Frank Reich found himself on the wrong end of a 28-3 halftime scoreline. The situation became bleaker when Reich threw an interception that was returned for a touchdown, giving Houston a 35-3 lead. Buffalo's quest for a third straight Super Bowl appearance was in tatters. Cue the greatest comeback in NFL history as Reich threw four touchdown passes to steal an improbable 38-35 lead. Houston tied the game with a late field goal, but the Bills won 41-38 in overtime on Steve Christie's match-winning 32-yard kick. Recalling the famous comeback, Reich said: 'When you're down by 32 points, you can't just be good on offense or defense – you've got to be good in every area and you've got to make big plays in every area. That happened and we were nearly flawless for almost half of the game.' Buffalo's 32-point comeback stood as an NFL record for almost 30 years.

★ DID YOU KNOW? ★

Buffalo's legendary fan base is known as 'Bills Mafia'. The pre-game activities of the passionate supporters often see fans cover themselves in ketchup and mustard before jumping off step ladders and breaking picnic tables. Why? Only those involved can know for sure, but the colourful scene has become a part of Buffalo's NFL Sundays.

CINCINNATI BENGALS

FIRST SEASON
1968

DIVISION
AFC North

COLOURS
Black, orange and white

OWNER
Mike Brown

HEAD COACH
Zac Taylor

STADIUM
Paycor Stadium (65,515)

NFL TITLES/SUPER BOWLS:
0

CINCINNATI BENGALS

INTRODUCING THE BENGALS . . .

The Cincinnati Bengals are a distinctive team with tiger stripes on their helmets, and they have featured many stand-out players worthy of our attention since their first season in 1968. But the team, which is named after a rare white Bengal tiger that was housed at Cincinnati Zoo, is still awaiting its first Super Bowl success.

The Bengals have learned the hard way about sport's fine margins. In Super Bowl 16 (1981 season), Cincinnati lost 26-21 to the San Francisco 49ers. Those teams met again in Super Bowl 23 (1988 season) and the 49ers prevailed, scoring a John Taylor touchdown with just 34 seconds remaining to snatch a 20-16 win. And in Super Bowl 56 (2021 season), the Bengals were five minutes from their first Super Bowl victory before the Los Angeles Rams rallied for a 23-20 win.

A year later, Cincinnati reached the AFC Championship Game before falling to the Kansas City Chiefs by just three points. Hopes will remain high as long as all-star quarterback Joe Burrow is at the helm and healthy. The 28-year-old is one of the league's leading players and he was Cincinnati's biggest star in a 2024 season that saw the team win its final five games, only to narrowly miss out on the playoffs.

Burrow, who won the NFL's Comeback Player of the Year prize as he returned from a wrist injury that wiped out his 2023 campaign, led the league with 4,918 passing yards and 43 touchdown throws – both career highs. Burrow's favourite target is dangerous receiver Ja'Marr Chase, who became the highest-paid non-quarterback in NFL history in March 2025, inking a deal worth more than $40 million per year. With the Bengals also signing receiver Tee Higgins to an extension in that same month, the team is spending an average of $124 million per season on Burrow and his two favourite targets – more than 44 per cent of Cincinnati's annual salary cap. That trio make the Bengals must-watch TV every weekend and will be key to any future success.

HOME

PAYCOR STADIUM

Paycor Stadium has been the Bengals' home since 2000. Nestled on the banks of the Ohio River, its open corners allow for great views of Cincinnati's skyscrapers and bridges. In a Harris Interactive survey conducted in 2007, Paycor Stadium was the only American football venue to make a list of 'America's favourite 150 buildings and structures.' It is nicknamed 'The Jungle', and that means a regular blasting of Guns N' Roses classic 'Welcome to the Jungle' on gamedays.

HEAD COACH

ZAC TAYLOR

Zac Taylor is in his seventh season leading the Bengals, having become the 10th head coach in club history in 2019. Taylor guided Cincinnati to a winning record in three consecutive seasons from 2022, even when an injured Joe Burrow could only play in 10 of 17 games in 2023. Taylor got his NFL coaching break with the Miami Dolphins in 2012 and also worked for the Los Angeles Rams before taking charge in Cincinnati. As a former college football quarterback himself, Taylor has forged a reputation as a coach who brings out the best in his passers.

JOE BURROW – QUARTERBACK

From the moment he arrives at the stadium on gameday, Joe Burrow oozes star power and is one of the most colourful characters in the sport. While his bold fashion sense has become the talk of America and beyond, Burrow is much more than a walking, talking mannequin – he is one of the NFL's elite quarterbacks. And he knows it. While not arrogant by any means, Burrow has a steely confidence that spreads throughout his team. The cold-blooded defense-killer said: 'As a quarterback, I think it's really important to exude that confidence. The quarterback sets the tone for the culture in the locker room and I try to be that kind of player and person for everybody here.' Burrow is an extremely accurate passer and an athletic runner who frustrates defenders who think they have him in their grasp. But, above all, the son of long-time American football coach Jim Burrow is an ice-in-his-veins winner who barely sees his pulse rise in pressure situations. Since joining the Bengals in 2020, Burrow has led Cincinnati to one Super Bowl appearance and to another AFC Championship Game. Ultimate success is a realistic goal – Burrow has all the tools to end the Bengals' title drought.

ANTHONY MUNOZ – OFFENSIVE TACKLE

The Bengals have fielded a host of excellent athletes over the years, including quarterbacks Ken Anderson and Boomer Esiason, receivers Chad Ochocinco and A.J. Green, and cornerback Ken Riley, but they boast just two players in the Pro Football Hall of Fame and their first was offensive tackle Anthony Munoz. The first-round pick from 1980 was considered a gamble after undergoing three knee surgeries in college at Southern California. Would he last? Munoz did more than that, as he became a mainstay from 1980 to 1992, helping Cincinnati reach two Super Bowls. At his peak, Munoz was the league's dominant lineman – a brutal blocker on running plays and a quarterback's best and most protective friend on passes downfield. The 11-time all-star was everything the Bengals could have hoped for and more. Former Cincinnati head coach Sam Wyche once said of Munoz: 'This is what heroes are supposed to look and act like.'

THE FREEZER BOWL

The 1981 season's AFC Championship Game saw the Bengals advance to their first Super Bowl with a 27-7 win over the San Diego Chargers. Despite that scoreline, the victory was anything but routine as the game, played on 10 January 1982, became known as 'The Freezer Bowl' and was the second-coldest in NFL history.

The temperature at kick-off was -9 Fahrenheit with a wind chill of -32. There were unofficial wind chill readings as low as -59. After ignoring the pleas of Chargers owner Gene Klein to move the game to balmy San Diego, Cincinnati set an early tone as their offensive linemen participated in pre-game warmups in short-sleeved t-shirts, a layer of Vaseline being the only protection for arms exposed to the Arctic conditions.

Cincinnati fared much better than the visitors from California. Ken Anderson threw for 161 yards and two touchdowns, including an eight-yard scoring pass to tight end M.L. Harris, who made his vital catch while wearing regular winter gloves!

Bengals head coach Forrest Gregg, who had played in the coldest game ever as a player for the Green Bay Packers (see page 213), said: 'Our guys played like it was another game, as if it was a normal day. The way they executed in those conditions was just amazing.'

★ DID YOU KNOW? ★

The Bengals were formed by Paul Brown – a multi-championship-winning coach with the Cleveland Browns, who were named after him. One of American football's great innovators, responsible for film scouting, playbooks and facemasks on helmets, Brown was already in the Pro Football Hall of Fame before also serving as Cincinnati's first head coach from 1968 to 1975.

CLEVELAND BROWNS

FIRST SEASON
1946

DIVISION
AFC North

COLOURS
Brown, orange and white

OWNER
Jimmy and Dee Haslam

HEAD COACH
Kevin Stefanski

STADIUM
Huntington Bank Field (67,431)

NFL TITLES/SUPER BOWLS:
4 (1950, 1954, 1955, 1964)

INTRODUCING THE BROWNS . . .

The Cleveland Browns boast a long and illustrious history, but also a rather complicated one. The club was founded in 1944 and began playing in a rival league to the NFL, the All-America Football Conference, in 1946. Named after their first coach, Paul Brown, the young franchise dominated the AAFC by winning four straight league championships from 1946 to 1949.

When the AAFC folded, the Browns joined the NFL. Led by legendary quarterback Otto Graham, Cleveland played in six straight NFL title contests, taking their total to 10 championship game appearances in 10 years across two leagues. They were crowned NFL champions in 1950, 1954 and 1955. They added another title in 1964 when powered by superstar running back Jim Brown. But the Browns are one of four teams that have yet to play in a Super Bowl.

In 1995, owner Art Modell announced that the franchise would relocate to Baltimore in time for the 1996 season kick-off. But the NFL ruled that the illustrious Browns name, history and records should remain in Cleveland for any future return to the city. So, the old Browns became the Baltimore Ravens and the new Browns returned to the NFL in 1999, much to the delight of a passionate fan base that was the very reason the history and name had stayed in Cleveland.

After the Browns missed the playoffs for 17 straight seasons, from 2003 to 2019, there have been recent signs of competitiveness. The Browns reached the knockout tournament in 2020 and 2023 under two-time NFL Coach of the Year Kevin Stefanski.

HOME

Huntington Bank Field

The Browns' current home sits on the site of Cleveland Municipal Stadium, which hosted the team from 1946 to 1995. Debris from the old stadium serves as an artificial reef in nearby Lake Erie. Both stadiums have traditionally created a rabid atmosphere. The bleachers behind the east end zone are known as 'The Dawg Pound', after cornerback Hanford Dixon called his defensive teammates 'Dawgs' in 1985. It is home to some of the NFL's noisiest supporters.

HEAD COACH

KEVIN STEFANSKI

In his first five seasons in Cleveland, Kevin Stefanski was twice named NFL Coach of the Year. In 2020, the 43-year-old led the Browns to their first playoff berth since 2002 and their first postseason win since 1994. And in 2023, he guided Cleveland back to the playoffs with an 11-6 record, despite being forced to start five different quarterbacks during a testing campaign. Stefanski entered the NFL as assistant to Minnesota Vikings head coach Brad Childress, rising to oversee that team's offense in 2019 before leaving for Ohio. As well as his offensive play-calling prowess, Stefanski is an inspirational leader.

MYLES GARRETT – DEFENSIVE END

During preseason training camp in 2017, then-Cleveland Browns Executive Vice-President of Football Operations Sashi Brown paid tribute to the club's rookie defensive end Myles Garrett by saying: 'He is a superb athlete and as good an athlete as I've ever seen in any sport. He's going to give opposing quarterbacks a nightmare for a long time here under our helmet.' Those words have proven to be prophetic. Garrett, who was the first overall selection in the 2017 NFL Draft, is Cleveland's driving force and leads a defense that ranked first in the NFL in 2023. That season saw Garrett at his dominant best as he was voted NFL Defensive Player of the Year. In that same campaign, Pro Football Focus hailed Garrett as the best player in the NFL, regardless of position. It's easy to see why. The six-time all-star explodes off the snap and can either bend around or bull his way through linemen en route to the quarterback. And when he gets there, Garrett regularly delivers the big moment by recording a sack or forcing a fumble. In his first 100 NFL games, the explosive and disruptive Garrett recorded 88½ sacks (defenders share half a sack each if they both take down the quarterback at the same time) – third-most in league history. In March 2025, Garrett became the highest-paid defender in NFL history when he inked a new four-year deal worth $40 million per season.

JIM BROWN – RUNNING BACK

There are some who believe that Superman was not a popular comic book character from Krypton – he was a running back who wore number 32 for the Cleveland Browns and went by the name of Jim Brown. Such was the impact of the Hall of Famer, who starred from 1957 to 1965, leading the NFL in rushing yards in eight of his nine seasons. Brown was blessed with the body and power of a linebacker, but he boasted a sprinter's speed, forming the complete package to guide Cleveland to NFL glory in 1964. A star on and off the field, Brown surprisingly retired while in London shooting scenes for *The Dirty Dozen*. His legacy was secure. Fellow Hall of Famer, New York Giants linebacker Sam Huff, recalled: 'Jim Brown was a load. He was known in pro football as "The Big Man". He was unbelievable. He's the greatest football player I've ever seen.'

RE-INTEGRATING PROFESSIONAL FOOTBALL

Paul Brown was considered one of the greatest innovators in American football history and a true legend who shaped so much of the game we know and love today. One of his first acts as head coach of the Cleveland Browns changed the sport for the better and forever. He signed a pair of African-American prospects in powerful running back Marion Motley and hard-nosed defensive lineman Bill Willis, breaking American football's colour barrier and truly re-integrating the sport for the first time since the 1920s. While there were some Black players sprinkled across the NFL over the league's early years, most clubs were fielding all-white squads by the mid-thirties. Brown heralded significant change by adding two key performers for his championship-winning squads. Current Cincinnati Bengals owner Mike Brown, son of Paul, said: 'He didn't do it for any other reason than to make the team better. It wasn't to sell tickets in the sense of drawing people because we had a couple of Black guys on the team. He thought these were the best football players and they should have a chance to play.' Motley and Willis both became greats forever enshrined in the Pro Football Hall of Fame.

★ DID YOU KNOW? ★

The Cleveland Browns are the only NFL team not to feature a logo or any pattern on their (plain orange) helmets. The club began wearing all-white helmets in 1946 but switched to orange in 1951 when NFL rules stipulated that headgear had to contrast with the white footballs being used for night games.

DENVER BRONCOS

FIRST SEASON
1960

OWNER
Rob Walton

DIVISION
AFC West

HEAD COACH
Sean Payton

COLOURS
**Sunset orange,
midnight navy
and summit
white**

STADIUM
**Empower Field
at Mile High
(76,125)**

NFL TITLES/SUPER BOWLS:
**3 (1997, 1998,
2015)**

DENVER BRONCOS

INTRODUCING THE BRONCOS . . .

As the name of their stadium suggests, the Denver Broncos play a mile above sea level in Colorado's Rocky Mountains, and the geography of this team has been fitting because they have climbed to the very top of the NFL on three occasions, winning Super Bowls in the 1997, 1998 and 2015 seasons.

Those title wins at the end of the 1990s were eagerly awaited, because the Broncos had been one of the most popular and entertaining teams of the 1980s with the great John Elway at quarterback, but they came up empty-handed with Super Bowl losses in the 1986, 1987 and 1989 seasons.

In total, the Broncos – who spent their first 10 years in the rival American Football League before joining the NFL – have appeared in eight Super Bowls (second-most in NFL history), with their third win being led by another Hall of Fame quarterback in Peyton Manning. Ably supported by a dominant defense, the Broncos won the NFL's 50th Super Bowl in the 2015 season. Following that championship win, Denver missed the AFC playoffs in eight consecutive seasons – the first Super Bowl champion to suffer such a fate.

The Broncos ended that unwanted streak in 2024, as they won 10 games and returned to the playoffs for the 23rd time in team history. And the future now looks a great deal brighter for a team with answers at two pivotal positions.

The partnership between proven head coach Sean Payton, who won a Super Bowl when leading the New Orleans Saints, and 2024 first-round quarterback Bo Nix should mean the Broncos remain competitive for many years to come. In his rookie season in the NFL, Nix proved himself to be an all-action star who inspired those around him with his on-the-money throws and bold and adventurous runs. And he also showed himself to be capable of taking Payton's renowned hard-nosed coaching.

HOME

EMPOWER FIELD AT MILE HIGH

The Broncos are cheered on by some of the NFL's most boisterous fans and gamedays at Empower Field at Mile High are loud and very orange! While naming rights have changed over the years at the 76,125-seat venue, which opened on the site of the team's old stadium in 2001, the 'Mile High' moniker has remained as a nod to the fact the Broncos play at an altitude of 5,280 feet (exactly one mile) above sea level.

HEAD COACH

SEAN PAYTON

Sean Payton is a former quarterback who played for the Chicago Bears in 1987 before beginning his coaching career at San Diego State University in 1988. He first entered the NFL coaching ranks with the Philadelphia Eagles in 1997 and also worked for the New York Giants and Dallas Cowboys before becoming head coach of the New Orleans Saints in 2006. In New Orleans, Payton turned around a struggling franchise, masterminded one of the league's most potent attacks, won NFL Coach of the Year honours and led the Saints to their lone Super Bowl success in the 2009 season. An excellent tactician but also a strict, old-school disciplinarian, Payton took charge of the Broncos in 2023 and delivered a playoff berth in 2024.

PATRICK SURTAIN II – CORNERBACK

The AFC West division has a pair of strong-armed quarterbacks in Kansas City's Patrick Mahomes and Justin Herbert of the Los Angeles Chargers. So, the Broncos have armed themselves with one of the best pass defenders in the NFL in cornerback Patrick Surtain II. A product of the University of Alabama, he was chosen ninth in the 2021 NFL Draft and immediately began shutting down the league's best wide receivers on his way to being named one of the NFL's best rookies. In 2022, Surtain was voted to the NFL's Pro Bowl all-star game and was also named All-Pro – the league's best of the best. In 2024, Surtain took his game to another level and recorded four interceptions on his way to being named NFL Defensive Player of the Year. Surtain is big for his position at 6-foot-2 and 202 pounds, very fast and boasts a high football IQ, which allows him to read where quarterbacks are going with the ball. He is the son of former Miami Dolphins and Kansas City Chiefs cornerback Patrick Surtain, who was a three-time all-star himself.

JOHN ELWAY – QUARTERBACK

For 16 seasons, from 1983 to 1998, the Denver Broncos were led by a rare one-club man in John Elway, who also happened to be one of the greatest quarterbacks to grace the NFL. The Hall of Famer could frustrate defenders with his mobility, but his superpower was a right arm loaded with defense-splitting venom. It was often suggested that Elway could throw a football through a car wash without it getting wet – it was a skill that also saw him drafted as a pitcher for Major League Baseball's Kansas City Royals, but he didn't pursue that sport. Elway was originally drafted by the Baltimore Colts, but pulled a bold and rare move by refusing to play for them, initiating a trade to the Broncos. While frustrating for the Colts, it was the start of a beautiful relationship in Denver. Elway came up short in his first three Super Bowl appearances but delivered NFL titles right at the end of his career in the 1997 and 1998 seasons. Elway served as the club's general manager from 2011 to 2022 and built a Super Bowl championship team around Peyton Manning in the 2015 season, cementing his status as a Broncos legend.

THE HELICOPTER!

After losing three Super Bowls in four seasons, John Elway looked destined to be one of the game's 'nearly men'. But he and the Broncos worked their way into Super Bowl 32 in the 1997 season. Denver were not expected to win the contest against the favoured Green Bay Packers, but they knew their quarterback would give his absolute all. The game was tied at 17-17 late in the third quarter when Elway ran to pick up a key first down. The 37-year-old saw three Packers defenders converging and knew his only way to keep Denver's scoring chances alive was to go over them. So, he launched into a dive only to be hit by the trio of defenders, who sent him into a helicopter spin that instantly became one of the NFL's most iconic plays. Elway picked up the first down and, two plays later, Denver moved into a 24-17 lead on Terrell Davis' touchdown run. Elway hurt his ribs while being spun 360 degrees in the air, but he had turned the tide in his team's favour. He recalled: 'The first thing I did was look to our sideline and our whole sideline was going crazy. At that point, we knew we were not leaving that game without getting the victory.' The inspired Broncos did indeed go on to win 31-24, giving Elway his first Super Bowl ring.

★ DID YOU KNOW? ★

Broncos head coach Sean Payton played quarterback for the Leicester Panthers – an amateur team in the United Kingdom's Budweiser League in 1988. Payton said: 'John Grisham wrote a book about playing for pizza in Europe and, when I read that book, I felt like he was writing about me. I lived in Leicester for seven months and had some great experiences there. The people were great and it was fantastic.'

HOUSTON TEXANS

FIRST SEASON
2002

DIVISION
AFC South

COLOURS
Deep steel blue, battle red, liberty white

OWNER
Janice S. McNair and Cal McNair

HEAD COACH
DeMeco Ryans

STADIUM
NRG Stadium (72,220)

NFL TITLES/SUPER BOWLS:
0

INTRODUCING THE TEXANS . . .

The Houston Texans are the youngest team in the NFL, being awarded a franchise in 1999 and beginning play in 2002. They are the second NFL club to call Houston their home, with the Oilers playing in the city from 1970 to 1996 before leaving to become the Tennessee Titans.

It was a rough beginning for the Texans as they did not make the playoffs until their 10th season. They have qualified for the playoffs eight times in their history but have never made it past the NFL's final eight (Divisional Round).

Under the leadership of head coach DeMeco Ryans, the Texans are currently loaded with exciting young talent, which suggests they could go so far as to scratch their name off the list of four teams never to have played in a Super Bowl (Cleveland Browns, Detroit Lions and Jacksonville Jaguars being the others).

Quarterback C.J. Stroud is one of the biggest reasons for the increased optimism surrounding the Texans. Prior to his arrival in 2023, Houston had won just 11 games in the previous three seasons combined. As a rookie, Stroud led the Texans to 11 wins in a single year, guiding his team to the AFC South title with 10 regular season victories before engineering a 45-14 win over the Cleveland Browns in the playoffs. That trick was repeated in 2024 with another 10 regular season wins, a division title and a playoff victory over the Los Angeles Chargers.

After some testing times, which have seen the Texans often fail to find the right head coach-quarterback combination, the future looks much brighter in Houston with Ryans and Stroud leading the way.

HOME

NRG STADIUM

NRG Stadium opened in 2002 as the first NFL facility to feature a retractable roof. It can be opened or closed in seven minutes. The 72,220-seat venue hosted Super Bowl 38 (2003 season) and Super Bowl 51 (2016 season) – both won by the New England Patriots. NRG Stadium has hosted a wide range of events from Taylor Swift concerts to Monster Jam and Wrestlemania. The venue will host seven matches at the 2026 FIFA World Cup.

HEAD COACH

DeMECO RYANS

DeMeco Ryans played linebacker in the NFL for 10 seasons from 2006 to 2015, starring for the Houston Texans for six of those years. The 2006 NFL Defensive Rookie of the Year was a two-time all-star during his spell in Houston. After making 970 career tackles, Ryans retired in 2015 after a four-year stint with the Philadelphia Eagles. He became an assistant coach for the San Francisco 49ers in 2017, rising to oversee their defense before taking charge of Houston in 2023. The 41-year-old has quickly proven himself to be one of the NFL's most inspirational and influential young coaches.

C.J. STROUD – QUARTERBACK

In two AFC South-winning seasons, C.J. Stroud has established himself as one of the brightest and most-skilled quarterbacks in the NFL. It's not always been a glitzy life in the spotlight for Stroud, however. He had to overcome great personal adversity growing up in California and reportedly played youth games with old boots that gave him blisters and once wore just a single contact lens! The sky is now the limit for the 23-year-old who starred at Ohio State University before becoming the second overall pick in the 2023 NFL Draft. Stroud was named NFL Offensive Rookie of the Year in his debut season, as he out-performed the man chosen ahead of him in Carolina Panthers quarterback Bryce Young. Stroud boasts elite arm talent and the ability to frustrate defenders with athleticism and football intelligence. In his short time in the NFL, Stroud has also shown that no stage is too big. His star power, physical skills and calmness under pressure have drawn comparisons to three-time Super Bowl-winner Patrick Mahomes, of the Kansas City Chiefs. Like Mahomes, Stroud has raised expectation levels within his NFL city, re-awakening the passionate American football fans in Houston. The Super Bowl wins could also follow.

J.J. WATT – DEFENSIVE END

Houston's best period of success came in nine seasons from 2011 to 2019, when they reached the playoffs on six occasions. At the heart of that run was one of the NFL's greatest-ever defenders in defensive end J.J. Watt, who now spends his retirement at Turf Moor as a part-owner of Burnley F.C. Watt played 12 years in the NFL with 10 dominant campaigns in Houston from 2011 to 2020. The explosive and powerful star was a three-time NFL Defensive Player of the Year, harassing quarterbacks throughout his career with 114½ sacks. Watt was named to the league's All-Decade Team for the 2010s. He will have to wait until 2027 (five years after his retirement), but Watt – who was also named the NFL's Man of the Year in 2017 for his charitable work off the field – will certainly be inducted into the Pro Football Hall of Fame.

A FIRST PLAYOFF WIN

In their first eight years, the Texans posted a winning record just once, but failed to make the playoffs in that 2009 season. But the 2011 campaign brought long-awaited success in the form of 10 wins, a first AFC South division title and a home playoff game. After stumbling to three consecutive defeats at the end of the regular season, Houston rebounded to take advantage of their long-awaited moment in the spotlight, securing their first playoff victory with a 31-10 domination of the Cincinnati Bengals. Running back Arian Foster rushed for 153 yards and two touchdowns, then-rookie defensive end J.J. Watt registered an interception return touchdown, and wide receiver Andre Johnson scored on a 40-yard pass from third-string quarterback T.J. Yates, who was subbing for the injured Matt Schaub and Matt Leinart. Houston's defense, led by Watt, recorded four sacks and three interceptions of Bengals quarterback Andy Dalton. Johnson, who had been with the Texans since entering the NFL in 2003, said: 'This is something not just for me but for the whole organisation. It's a very special feeling.' Houston's season ended one week later with a defeat against the Baltimore Ravens, but they had finally logged a playoff victory.

★ DID YOU KNOW? ★

Texans defensive end Will Anderson Jr. has bullied and harassed opposing offensive linemen during his first two seasons in the NFL, earning all-star honours while recording 18 sacks. But as a younger brother to five older sisters growing up, it was Anderson on the receiving end of stressful situations. His sisters once famously locked him inside a tumble dryer. Ironic given that he is now the one putting offenses into a spin!

INDIANAPOLIS COLTS

FIRST SEASON
1953

DIVISION
AFC South

COLOURS
Speed blue, white, facemask grey and anvil black

OWNER
Carlie Irsay-Gordon, Casey Foyt and Kalen Jackson

HEAD COACH
Shane Steichen

STADIUM
Lucas Oil Stadium (63,000)

NFL TITLES/SUPER BOWLS:
4 (1958, 1959, 1970, 2006)

INDIANAPOLIS COLTS

INTRODUCING THE COLTS . . .

The history of the Colts spans seven decades and has seen the team with the iconic horseshoe on its helmet play in three stadiums in two cities, while competing in three different divisions. It is a legacy that has seen the Colts win four league titles – most recently at the end of the 2006 season – and one that includes some of the greatest figures in NFL history.

The Colts, who played in Baltimore from 1953 until a controversial middle-of-the-night departure to Indianapolis in 1984, have fielded outstanding quarterbacks over the years. Johnny Unitas played for the Colts from 1956 to 1972, reaching 10 Pro Bowl all-star games. He won three league MVP awards and three NFL titles. Peyton Manning was a 14-time all-star while leading one of the NFL's best attacks in Indianapolis from 1998–2011. Andrew Luck led the Colts from 2012 to 2018 and was voted to four Pro Bowls.

Manning turned the Colts into an NFL powerhouse at the turn of the century, delivering nine straight playoff berths from 2002–2010, winning a Super Bowl in 2006 and appearing in another three years later.

The Colts missed the playoffs for four straight seasons from 2021 but came within one victory of qualifying in 2023 under the leadership of head coach Shane Steichen. He boasts an exciting squad ready to mount a challenge. Quarterback Anthony Richardson, former NFL rushing champion Jonathan Taylor and electrifying wide receiver Alec Pierce are game-changing talents capable of putting the Colts back in the AFC playoff race.

HOME

LUCAS OIL STADIUM

Opened in 2008, Lucas Oil Stadium features a retractable roof that can open or close in approximately 11 minutes and a giant window that offers spectacular views of downtown Indianapolis. The 63,000-seat venue played host to Super Bowl 46 in the 2011 season. The stadium also hosts the annual NFL Combine and has served as the venue for a wide range of artists, from Taylor Swift to U2 and One Direction to Guns N' Roses.

HEAD COACH

SHANE STEICHEN

A former quarterback at the University of Nevada, Las Vegas, Shane Steichen began his tenure at the Colts in 2023. When a dislocated ankle and broken leg ended his playing career at UNLV, Steichen said: 'All right, I'm onto my coaching career.' After spells with the Los Angeles Chargers, Cleveland Browns and Philadelphia Eagles, Steichen led the Colts to a winning record in his first season. Steichen is laying firm foundations in Indianapolis, as he explained: 'Culture is a huge part of any organisation but especially in sports. The four pillars I preach every day are character, preparation, consistency and relentlessness.'

ZAIRE FRANKLIN – LINEBACKER

It's fair to say that things have clicked into place for Colts linebacker Zaire Franklin and he has grown to become one of the league's most impactful defenders. In his first four seasons in the NFL, Franklin – who was chosen by the Colts in the seventh and final round of the 2018 Draft – recorded a total of just 94 tackles and only occasionally featured on defense. In the three years that followed, Franklin morphed into a tackling machine and registered an incredible 519 stops. He was named as a Pro Bowl all-star in 2024. With an elite mix of speed and power, Franklin runs like the wind and hits like a runaway freight train. He led the NFL with 173 tackles in 17 games in 2024. It was the third year in a row he made more than 167 tackles in a season. Whether he is stopping running backs in their tracks, chasing down quarterbacks or covering tight ends on passes downfield, Franklin gets the job done. He makes sure everyone knows about his playmaking prowess as Indy's emotional leader. Colts defensive end Kwity Paye said: 'He's a dog! I don't feel like our defense really talks trash. But "Z" is the one who is there talking trash with everybody.'

PEYTON MANNING – QUARTERBACK

The Colts were led by an NFL legend for 14 seasons from 1998 to 2011. Peyton Manning – the first pick in the 1998 NFL Draft – was one of the sport's most prolific and most intelligent quarterbacks. Known as 'The Sheriff' for his ability to lay down the law to opponents, Manning served as an extra coach on the field. He played in two Super Bowls with the Colts, winning on his first visit in 2006. In 2012, Manning joined the Denver Broncos and secured another two Super Bowl appearances, winning a second title in the final game of his career in 2015. Manning holds two key records to this day, having set single season passing marks for yards (5,477) and touchdowns (55) in 2013. Manning won a record five NFL Most Valuable Player awards, is a member of the Hall of Fame and is now a successful TV analyst for ESPN.

COLTS REIGN AS IT POURS

With Peyton Manning at quarterback, Hall of Famers Marvin Harrison and Reggie Wayne at receiver, and all-star Dallas Clark at tight end, the 2006 Colts fielded one of the league's best attacks and they reached a Super Bowl for the first time since 1970. Indianapolis faced the Chicago Bears in Super Bowl 41 in Miami. Both teams were expecting good weather conditions in Florida but instead had to battle through torrential rain and stormy winds. Clark recalled: 'Usually in Florida it pours for 15 minutes and then it's gone. But this cloud hung right over the stadium. It really became a ground game.' The Colts made the worst of starts as Chicago's Devin Hester returned the opening kick-off 92 yards for a touchdown. By the end of the first quarter, the Bears led 14-6. But the Colts worked their way back into the contest either side of a halftime show that, fittingly, featured Prince singing 'Purple Rain'. Manning only threw one touchdown pass but the Colts displayed their all-around strength by rushing for 191 yards and a touchdown, while also scoring on Kelvin Hayden's interception return. Indianapolis held the Bears to just one offensive touchdown in a hard-fought 29-17 win.

★ DID YOU KNOW? ★

The Colts have seen Weeb Ewbank, Don Shula, Ted Marchibroda and Tony Dungy win NFL Coach of the Year honours. Of that outstanding quartet of head coaches, only Marchibroda is not in the Pro Football Hall of Fame.

JACKSONVILLE JAGUARS

FIRST SEASON
1995

OWNER
Shahid Khan

DIVISION
AFC South

HEAD COACH
Liam Coen

COLOURS
Teal, black and gold

STADIUM
EverBank Stadium (67,814)

NFL TITLES/SUPER BOWLS:
0

JACKSONVILLE JAGUARS

INTRODUCING THE JAGUARS . . .

The Jaguars are one of the NFL's youngest teams, beginning play in 1995. They are one of four teams never to have played in a Super Bowl (the others being the Cleveland Browns, Detroit Lions and Houston Texans), but they have come close over the past three decades.

Jacksonville fell one win short of the Super Bowl – in the AFC Championship Game – during the 1996, 1999 and 2017 campaigns. And led by star quarterback Trevor Lawrence, the Jags were one of the final eight teams chasing Super Bowl glory in 2022 before falling to the eventual champions in the Kansas City Chiefs.

The Jaguars have reached the playoffs eight times in their history and boast enough talent to suggest they can mount more postseason challenges in the coming years. Lawrence is an exciting franchise leader at quarterback and he remains the key to future success. Tank Bigsby is a powerful and growing running back, while the passing attack is fuelled by one of the star wide receivers of the 2024 season in Brian Thomas Jr., and the defense features a pair of quarterback-disruptors in Josh Hines-Allen and Travon Walker.

The Jags are popular on both sides of the Atlantic, as they continue to grow their fan base in the UK thanks to their annual commitment to playing in London. Jacksonville have been playing regular season games at Wembley Stadium and Tottenham Hotspur Stadium since 2013. The 2025 season will see the Jaguars feature in a London game for the 14th time.

EVERBANK STADIUM

The Jaguars play at EverBank Stadium, which features an outdoor swimming pool perched above one of the end zones and luxurious kennels where fans can drop their dogs while watching games. The venue has played host to one Super Bowl at the end of the 2004 season. The Jaguars and the city of Jacksonville have agreed to renovations costing $1.4 billion in order to unveil a 63,000-seat 'Stadium of the Future' that will open in 2028.

LIAM COEN

Former college quarterback Liam Coen (Massachusetts) has been one of the fastest-rising assistant coaches in the NFL in recent years. He was named as Jaguars head coach in January 2025, after guiding one of the league's most potent attacks during the 2024 season as offensive coordinator of the Tampa Bay Buccaneers. Coen not only coaxed the best year of his career out of Bucs quarterback Baker Mayfield, he also turned the league's worst rushing attack into one of the very best. The 39-year-old got his NFL coaching break with the Los Angeles Rams in 2018, serving as assistant wide receivers coach. He oversaw their attack as offensive coordinator in 2022. As well as being considered an astute tactician, Coen is a positive culture-setter renowned for having strong relationships with his players.

TREVOR LAWRENCE – QUARTERBACK

While they have playmakers across their roster, the Jaguars are driven by strong-armed and accurate quarterback Trevor Lawrence. After an illustrious college career at Clemson University, Lawrence's NFL arrival was eagerly anticipated and he was the first player chosen in the 2021 Draft. Lawrence won his first NFL game in London, leading Jacksonville to a 23-20 victory over the Miami Dolphins. And in 2022, Lawrence earned Pro Bowl all-star honours as Jacksonville won the AFC South Division. Once in that postseason tournament, Lawrence excelled by throwing four touchdown passes to lead Jacksonville to a 31-30 victory over the Los Angeles Chargers having trailed 27-0 in the first half. Delivering in such a big moment surprised few in Jacksonville. Then-head coach Doug Pederson said: 'That shows a lot of his character, who he is as a player and who he is as a person. He's the real deal.' It has not been plain sailing for Lawrence, however, who missed seven games in 2024 with a shoulder injury and a concussion. And Liam Coen will be his third head coach in five seasons. But if Lawrence can settle into a groove with his new leader, the Jaguars will be in safe hands with their athletic and gifted quarterback.

TONY BOSELLI – OFFENSIVE TACKLE

The Jacksonville Jaguars hit a home run when making the first draft pick in team history in 1995. University of Southern California offensive tackle Tony Boselli was a beast of an offensive lineman, a gem of a man and one of the greatest players in NFL history. The 6-foot-7, 322-pound giant was the cornerstone of a Jacksonville team that shocked the football world by reaching the playoffs in four of their first five seasons. Boselli was as mean and intimidating as he was athletic. A shoulder injury limited the five-time Pro Bowler to just 91 games over seven seasons, but he absolutely dominated the greatest defensive linemen of his era. And in 2022, after being a finalist six times, Boselli joined American football's greatest team and will go down forever as one of the best to ever play the game after being inducted into the Pro Football Hall of Fame. Now, Boselli is guiding the Jaguars into a new era having been named the team's Executive Vice President of Football Operations in 2025. The position sees Boselli overseeing all major football-related decisions in Jacksonville, and one of his first tasks was to hire head coach Liam Coen and general manager James Gladstone.

A FIRST WIN IN LONDON

When the Jaguars arrived in London to play the Buffalo Bills in 2015, they were desperate to change their fortunes in the English capital, having been handily beaten by the San Francisco 49ers and Dallas Cowboys in 2013 and 2014. And it looked like their attempt at third time lucky was going to be a comfortable stroll in front of a sold-out crowd at Wembley Stadium. The Jaguars stormed into a commanding 27-3 lead by scoring on an Allen Robinson catch, a T.J. Yeldon run and defensive touchdowns from Chris Clemons and Telvin Smith. But it was not commanding enough. Buffalo frantically fought back, moving into a 31-27 lead on Corey Graham's 44-yard interception return with just over five minutes left in the game. Jaguars quarterback Blake Bortles had one final chance to make amends for his mistake. And he did just that, throwing an inch-perfect 31-yard touchdown pass to Allen Hurns for a 34-31 victory. Hurns laid out horizontally at full stretch three feet in the air before reeling in the winning throw, landing face-first on the ground and coming up with chunks of Wembley turf all over his face. Hurns later revealed that he was allergic to grass! But he had no complaints on that historic day in London.

★ DID YOU KNOW? ★

Former Gloucester and Wales rugby union star Louis Rees-Zammit is a member of the Jacksonville Jaguars. After switching sports and spending just 10 weeks on the NFL's International Player Pathway programme early in 2024, Rees-Zammit was signed as a running back by the Kansas City Chiefs. After being released by that team at the end of 2024 training camp, 'Rees Lightning' joined the Jags as a wide receiver and spent the regular season with the AFC South club. Rees-Zammit signed a new contract with the Jaguars in February 2025.

KANSAS CITY CHIEFS

FIRST SEASON
1960

OWNER
Clark Hunt

DIVISION
AFC West

HEAD COACH
Andy Reid

COLOURS
Red, gold and white

STADIUM
Arrowhead Stadium (76,416)

NFL TITLES/SUPER BOWLS:
4 (1969, 2019, 2022, 2023)

KANSAS CITY CHIEFS

INTRODUCING THE CHIEFS . . .

The Kansas City Chiefs are the gold standard when it comes to recent NFL success. The franchise that played its first three seasons as the Dallas Texans before moving to Kansas City and changing its name has appeared in five of the last six Super Bowls. They won three of those title games in the 2019, 2022 and 2023 seasons. Those last two victories saw Kansas City become the NFL's first repeat champions since the New England Patriots in 2003 and 2004.

The Chiefs are powered by one of the best head coach-quarterback partnerships in NFL history with Andy Reid calling the plays for his superstar passer, Patrick Mahomes. Prior to the arrival of the influential duo, the Chiefs had not come close to winning a Super Bowl since doing so at the end of the 1969 season – their only other success. While he is universally regarded as the best player in the NFL, Mahomes is not a one-man team and the 2023 and 2024 seasons saw Kansas City's runs to the Super Bowl inspired by one of the best young defenses in the league.

Cheering on the Chiefs is one of the most passionate crowds in any sport. In 2014, Chiefs fans set a new Guinness World Record for making the most noise in an outdoor stadium, registering 142.2 decibels – that's louder than a jet plane on take-off! The supporters, known as 'Chiefs Kingdom', are loud and Mahomes and his teammates give them every reason to be proud.

HOME

ARROWHEAD STADIUM

This iconic 76,416-seat open-air bowl of a stadium filled with striking red seats is on the bucket list of most NFL fans. Gamedays at Arrowhead Stadium are filled with barbecues at pre-game tailgate parties, passionate fans and memorable moments on the field. The venue, which opened in 1972, will host four group matches, one round of 32 game and a quarter-final at the 2026 FIFA World Cup.

HEAD COACH

ANDY REID

The Chiefs are led by one of the most imaginative and successful head coaches in NFL history in Andy Reid. The 67-year-old, who is reported to be the league's highest-paid coach, is a renowned play-caller and tactical mastermind. 'Big Red' is the only coach in NFL history to win at least 100 games with two different teams. The former college offensive lineman served as coach of the Philadelphia Eagles from 1999–2012, guiding that team to a Super Bowl appearance in the 2004 season. He took charge of the Chiefs in 2013 and has won a hat-trick of Vince Lombardi Trophies.

PATRICK MAHOMES – QUARTERBACK

Patrick Mahomes is the NFL's biggest superstar. The quarterback chosen by the Chiefs in the first round of the 2017 NFL Draft is only 30 years old, but he has already won three Super Bowls and was named the game's Most Valuable Player in each of those victories. Mahomes has twice been selected as the NFL's MVP, signed a contract worth $500 million over 10 years, and has been voted an all-star in six of his first seven seasons as a starter. Mahomes is a magician with a football. He can throw traditional balls with his powerful right arm, but he has also been known to toss left-handed and no-look passes to attack defenses that often have no answer for his improvisational skills. Mahomes is also an excellent athlete who could have played Major League Baseball like his father, Pat, and he regularly makes key runs away from pressure. Perhaps Mahomes' greatest skill is his will to win. Like so many greats, Mahomes never knows when he is beaten. In each of his Super Bowl wins, the Chiefs have trailed by at least 10 points and their star man has still dragged them back to victory.

TONY GONZALEZ – TIGHT END

The Chiefs boast one of the greatest tight ends in recent NFL history in Travis Kelce, and they can also lay claim to one of the best the league has ever seen in Tony Gonzalez. The silky-smooth athlete who played one season of summer league basketball for the NBA's Miami Heat used those skills to box out defenders and make spectacular catches in a record-setting career in which he reeled in 1,325 passes (most for an NFL tight end) for 15,127 yards (also most for a tight end) and 111 touchdowns (second-most for a tight end). Gonzalez played 17 seasons, from 1997 to 2013. In his 12-year spell with the Chiefs from 1997 to 2008, he went to 10 Pro Bowl all-star games. Gonzalez was voted into the Pro Football Hall of Fame at the first time of asking in 2019. Later that year, he was named to the NFL's 100th Anniversary all-time team.

JET CHIP WASP

Half a century had passed since the Chiefs had won a Super Bowl when they faced the San Francisco 49ers at the end of the 2019 season. And the long wait for championship glory looked set to continue as San Francisco led 20-10 with just under nine minutes remaining.

Things looked bleak for Patrick Mahomes as he and the Chiefs faced a third-and-15 situation: a very low-percentage situation for any offense. Failure in this key moment would hand the Super Bowl to the 49ers. Super-computers whirred out predictions and San Francisco's win probability soared to more than 96 per cent.

Never tell Mahomes the odds.

The play called 'Jet Chip Wasp' saw Tyreek Hill get open deep downfield. Could Mahomes get him the ball? Under fierce pressure, Mahomes backed up 14 yards behind the line and threw the ball more than 57 yards through the air – his longest distance of the season. Hill reeled in the pass for a 44-yard gain. The famous play set up a Mahomes touchdown pass to Travis Kelce with 6:13 remaining.

The comeback was on. The 49ers were shocked and the Chiefs quickly scored two additional touchdowns to run out 31-20 winners. 'Jet Chip Wasp' was not only considered the turning point in that Super Bowl, it was also the moment a dynasty, a period of dominance, was born. The Chiefs have since gone on to appear in four more Super Bowls, winning two of them.

★ DID YOU KNOW? ★

American actor and *Modern Family* star Eric Stonestreet, who plays Cam in the hit sitcom, is a huge Kansas City Chiefs fan. He bears a resemblance to head coach Andy Reid and can often be found at Chiefs home games or preseason training camps impersonating the head coach.

LAS VEGAS RAIDERS

FIRST SEASON
1960

DIVISION
AFC West

COLOURS
Silver and black

OWNER
Mark Davis

HEAD COACH
Pete Carroll

STADIUM
Allegiant Stadium (65,000)

NFL TITLES/SUPER BOWLS:
3 (1976, 1980, 1983)

LAS VEGAS RAIDERS

INTRODUCING THE RAIDERS . . .

Kitted out in their iconic silver and black uniforms, the Raiders are one of the NFL's most recognisable teams. They are also among the most nomadic, having played in Oakland, Los Angeles, Oakland (again) and Las Vegas since their formation in 1960.

The Raiders became one of the NFL's most popular teams in the 1970s, when they were as controversial off the field as they were on it. The Silver and Black's roster was filled with colourful characters who partied as hard as they played, but few complained because they were winners.

In an 11-season period from 1967 to 1977, the Raiders qualified for the playoffs 10 times and won a Super Bowl during the 1976 campaign, when led by legendary head coach John Madden, quarterback Kenny Stabler and one of the most dominant defenses in league history. At one point during that run, the Raiders played in five straight AFC Championship Games.

The Raiders added two more Super Bowl titles in the 1980 and 1983 seasons, but they have not played in the big game since losing to the Tampa Bay Buccaneers at the end of the 2002 campaign. The modern-day Raiders have fallen on harder times and have missed the playoffs repeatedly in the past decade.

But under the leadership of new part-owner Tom Brady – the greatest player in NFL history – the Raiders will be hoping to develop the kind of winning habits perfected by the quarterback during his own playing days with the New England Patriots and Tampa Bay Buccaneers. For that to happen, the new leadership pairing of head coach Pete Carroll and quarterback Geno Smith will need to click as they did when they were together in Seattle in 2022. During that campaign, Smith threw a career-high 30 touchdown passes and delivered a spot in the NFC playoffs in his first meaningful NFL action in eight seasons.

ALLEGIANT STADIUM

The Raiders play at futuristic Allegiant Stadium, which sits a stone's throw south-west of the world-famous Las Vegas Strip. Nicknamed 'The Death Star' because of its silver and black exterior, the domed 65,000-seat venue opened in 2020. The stadium, which played host to Super Bowl 58 at the end of the 2023 season, features a grass field that can be rolled in and out on a giant tray.

PETE CARROLL

Pete Carroll has been one of the most successful coaches in recent NFL history, consistently turning out a competitive team during his tenure with the Seattle Seahawks from 2010 to 2023. In 14 seasons leading the Seahawks, his teams reached the playoffs 10 times and qualified for two Super Bowls in 2013 and 2014. They were victorious in the first of those title games, defeating the Denver Broncos 43-8 in Super Bowl 48. Carroll – who began his career as a defensive expert – is a high-energy leader who defies his years. The former New York Jets (1994) and New England Patriots (1997–1999) head coach turned 74 one week into the 2025 season. Upon coaching his first game with the Raiders, Carroll became the oldest head coach in NFL history.

MAXX CROSBY – DEFENSIVE END

American football is the ultimate team game, with success often determined by all 11 players on the field doing their jobs to a high level at the same time. There are no one-man attacks or defenses in the NFL, although the Raiders test that theory to its limits when it comes to pass-rushing phenomenon Maxx Crosby. Nicknamed 'The Condor', due to his long arms and wingspan, which can fend off opposing blockers before swallowing up quarterbacks for sacks, Crosby has become the driving force of the Raiders. Crosby's greatest attributes are his desire to succeed and his passion for the game. It may sound like a cliché, but the three-time all-star attacks every play like it's his last. And that approach has served him well, particularly in a 2023 campaign, when Crosby recorded a career-high 14½ sacks. The fourth-round draft pick from 2019 plays with great confidence, admitting: 'Every time I go out there, I feel like I'm unstoppable.' Plenty would agree. Cleveland Browns superstar pass rusher Myles Garrett said: 'I love Maxx. He plays the game with a hell of a motor.' Former Miami Dolphins all-star offensive tackle Terron Armstead added: 'He is relentless. The dude is insane.' Crosby was rewarded for his efforts in March 2025, as he signed a new deal worth $35.5 million per year, briefly making him the highest-paid defender in NFL history before being passed by Garrett.

MARCUS ALLEN – RUNNING BACK

There was a period of time in the 1980s when running backs were often as important to their teams as quarterbacks. During that decade, the league featured greats such as Walter Payton, Eric Dickerson and John Riggins. From 1982 to 1992, the Raiders had a star of their own in Marcus Allen, who finished his career with a five-year spell in Kansas City. Allen led those teams in rushing 11 times during a career that saw him inducted into the Pro Football Hall of Fame in 2003. Allen was athletic, but he was also willing to gain the hard yards and was one of the best goal-line and short yardage backs in the game. His finest night came in Super Bowl 18 against Washington to cap the 1983 season. In a dominant 38-9 win, Allen rushed for 191 yards and two touchdowns. His 74-yard scoring run was one of the greatest in Super Bowl history. Allen took the ball and headed left, only to be met by two Washington defenders who were about to drop him for a big loss. The six-time all-star turned and started running to the right, shrugging off a defender hanging on his back before darting through the line and all the way to the end zone.

MOMENT IN TIME

THE SEA OF HANDS

In the 1974 season's AFC playoffs, the Raiders trailed the Miami Dolphins 26-21 with 35 seconds left in the game. Quarterback Kenny Stabler had every intention of throwing a strong and accurate pass from the Miami eight-yard line, but he was tripped by a Dolphins defender and could only loft a weak effort towards the goal-line as he fell face-first to the ground. The ball travelled through a 'sea of hands' created by three Miami defenders, and running back Clarence Davis caught it and held on for dear life as he was surrounded by enemy players. Touchdown, Raiders! Game over! Former Raiders personnel executive Ron Wolf later told NFL Films: 'Of all the players on the team who were eligible receivers, the one guy you wouldn't want to throw the ball to was Clarence Davis because he had boards for hands. But in that moment, he had the softest, surest hands in the history of the game.'

★ DID YOU KNOW? ★

The Raiders were once led by a head coach in John Madden, who enjoyed a remarkable American football career. He briefly played for the Philadelphia Eagles in 1959 and led the Raiders from 1969 to 1978, never having a losing season (having more losses than wins by the end of the regular season), winning a team record 103 games and one Super Bowl. Madden went on to win 16 Emmys as a legendary NFL commentator and also lent his name and expertise to the *Madden NFL* video game series, reaching a whole new generation of NFL fans.

LOS ANGELES CHARGERS

FIRST SEASON
1960

DIVISION
AFC West

COLOURS
**Powder blue,
sunshine gold
and white**

OWNER
Dean Spanos

HEAD COACH
Jim Harbaugh

STADIUM
**SoFi Stadium
(71,500)**

NFL TITLES/SUPER BOWLS:
0

INTRODUCING THE CHARGERS . . .

The Chargers began playing in the NFL's rival American Football League in 1960 under the ownership of Hilton Hotels heir Barron Hilton. They spent one season in Los Angeles before moving down the California coast to San Diego, where they would spend the next 56 seasons.

The Chargers enjoyed one championship-winning season in the AFL in 1963 before joining the NFL when the two leagues merged in 1970. Since then, the club has failed to win a Super Bowl. They reached the big game in the 1994 season but lost Super Bowl 29 by a score of 49-26 to the San Francisco 49ers.

The quarterback position features prominently in Chargers history, as they have fielded some big-name passers, such as Hall of Famer Dan Fouts and another pair of all-time greats in Drew Brees and Philip Rivers. Their current head coach, Jim Harbaugh, is a former Chargers quarterback and their leading man today is Pro Bowl all-star Justin Herbert, who possesses one of the strongest arms in the league.

In the battle to win fans in Los Angeles, the Chargers may be running slightly behind the Rams, who won a Super Bowl as recently as the 2021 season. But with Harbaugh and Herbert leading the way, the Chargers are definitely a team on the rise, as evidenced by their return to the NFL playoffs in the 2024 season.

HOME

SoFi STADIUM

The Chargers play home games at SoFi Stadium, which opened in 2020 and is owned by the Los Angeles Rams. The state-of-the-art venue is open-ended but has a fixed-roof canopy covering its 71,500 seats. The jewel in the crown of NFL stadia hosted Super Bowl 56 in the 2021 season and will host Super Bowl 61 in the 2026 campaign. It will also host the opening ceremony for the 2028 Olympic Games in Los Angeles.

HEAD COACH

JIM HARBAUGH

Former NFL quarterback Jim Harbaugh played for four teams over 14 seasons from 1987 to 2000. As a coach who preaches for his players to be tough and together, Harbaugh has been a serial winner. He led the 49ers from 2011 to 2014 and did not having a losing season. He took his team to the NFC Championship Game (Super Bowl semi-finals) in each of his first three seasons and guided San Francisco to a Super Bowl appearance in the 2012 campaign. After leaving that team in 2014, Harbaugh spent the following nine years as head coach at the University of Michigan, winning a national championship in 2023. Upon being hired by the Chargers in 2024, the quirky 61-year-old chose not to stay in a 5-star hotel while searching for a house. Instead, Harbaugh opted to live in his motorhome, which he parked on LA's Huntington Beach for several months. The veteran coach delivered 11 victories and a playoff berth in his first season with the Chargers.

STAR MAN

JUSTIN HERBERT – QUARTERBACK

At 6-foot-6 and boasting a power-packed arm, Justin Herbert has the look of a classic NFL quarterback who can stand behind his offensive line and deliver accurate fastballs downfield. But what makes Herbert the complete package and one of the NFL's brightest stars is the fact that, when required, he can use his speed and athleticism to run away from defenders and he plays tough every week. The Chargers selected Herbert with the sixth overall pick in the 2020 NFL Draft and he has lived up to that lofty selection with high-level performances. Herbert enjoyed a career-defining year in 2021, as he became the first player in Chargers history to throw for more than 5,000 yards in a season. And he led Los Angeles to the playoffs in 2022 and 2024. Herbert's biggest fan is his own head coach in Harbaugh, who said on *The Herd with Colin Cowherd*: 'There's nobody better. He's incredible. Every day when we go out for practice, we're around greatness. This is what greatness looks like. I sit at my desk and think, "Justin is on our team. Yes!" ' Herbert threw for 21,093 yards from 2020 to 2024 – the most of any quarterback in NFL history through his first five years in the league.

PHILIP RIVERS – QUARTERBACK

Philip Rivers never had a textbook throwing motion. His unorthodox sidearm came from throwing adult-sized footballs that he couldn't properly grip as a young boy while his father was coaching high-school American football. But Rivers proved himself to be one of NFL history's most prolific passers and is widely considered the greatest quarterback never to play in a Super Bowl. Rivers played 17 seasons, from 2004 to 2020, with the first 16 spent with the Chargers, where he was named a Pro Bowl all-star eight times. Rivers was as tough as he was talented. In the 2007 season's AFC Championship Game, Rivers played through the entirety of a defeat to the New England Patriots with torn knee ligaments that required offseason surgery. Rivers always played with a youthful exuberance, as he explained in an interview towards the end of his career: 'I play the game as I did when I was a 10-year-old in North Alabama in the back yard. I like to play with that demeanour – it's still a game. We are grown men playing a game.' Rivers has carried his passion into a post-NFL career, as he currently serves as head coach at St. Michael Catholic High School in Fairhope, Alabama.

WINSLOW'S BIG NIGHT

Kellen Winslow is worthy of his place in the Pro Football Hall of Fame, as he caught 541 passes in nine seasons with the Chargers from 1979 to 1987. But if you required further evidence of his greatness, you should watch highlights of the Chargers' win over the Miami Dolphins in the 1981 playoffs. On a steamy night in South Florida, Winslow put his body on the line. With the temperature north of 86 degrees Fahrenheit, Winslow was instrumental in his team's 41-38 overtime win, setting a playoff record with 13 catches for 166 yards. He battled through a bruised shoulder, a stitched lip, leg cramps, dehydration and twice had to replace his shoulder pads as they were broken by big hits. With the game tied at 38-38 and with Miami lining up to attempt a winning field goal in the final seconds, Winslow burst through the line to block the only kick of his career. The Chargers won in overtime with a field goal of their own. Winslow had nothing left to as he had to be helped off the field by teammates. The dehyrdrated and cramping star was estimated to have lost 13 pounds during the historic game and later admitted: 'I've never felt so close to death before. That's what Muhammad Ali said in Manila and that's how I felt there at the end.'

★ DID YOU KNOW? ★

For three seasons, from 1986 to 1988, the Chargers were led by an English head coach in Al Saunders. The native of Hendon, Middlesex, won 17 games and lost 22 during his spell in charge. His great-uncle, Ron Saunders, was a football manager for a host of clubs, including Manchester City and Aston Villa.

MIAMI DOLPHINS

FIRST SEASON
1966

DIVISION
AFC East

COLOURS
Aqua, orange, white and marine blue

OWNER
Stephen M. Ross

HEAD COACH
Mike McDaniel

STADIUM
Hard Rock Stadium (64,767)

NFL TITLES/SUPER BOWLS:
2 (1972, 1973)

INTRODUCING THE DOLPHINS . . .

The Miami Dolphins are one of the most popular NFL teams around the world thanks, in large part, to the exploits of legendary quarterback Dan Marino, who was one of the league's biggest stars in the 1980s and 1990s. While Marino never won a Super Bowl, his attacking and explosive style of play made the Dolphins a must-watch team.

Still closely associated with the franchise, Marino would approve of the modern iteration of the Dolphins. Miami boast one of the fastest and most explosive attacks in the entire league, utilising a variety of defense-busting options who would not look out of place running the 100 metres in the Olympics.

A speedy attack that pulls defenders in different directions and forces opponents to make split-second decisions is the brainchild of head coach Mike McDaniel, who guided Miami to the playoffs in each of his first two seasons after taking charge in 2022. But the Dolphins fell short in both knockout tournaments and have still not won a playoff game since the 2000 season. Their second and most recent Super Bowl success came in the 1973 campaign. So, Miami's fan base is starving for success.

The Dolphins have enough firepower to at least dream of reaching the Super Bowl for a sixth time, with Tua Tagovailoa delivering his trademark accurate passes at quarterback, explosive running backs De'Von Achane and Jaylen Wright capable of scoring from anywhere on the field, and track-speed wide receivers in Tyreek Hill and Jaylen Waddle blowing past defenders to make big catches downfield.

HARD ROCK STADIUM

Hard Rock Stadium has been the Dolphins' home since 1987. The venue underwent a $350 million renovation in 2015 that resulted in the majority of previously exposed seats being covered by an open-air canopy. The site has hosted six Super Bowls, most recently in the 2019 season as the Kansas City Chiefs defeated the San Francisco 49ers. Hard Rock also hosts a Formula 1 Grand Prix and will accommodate seven games at the 2026 FIFA World Cup.

MIKE McDANIEL

Mike McDaniel's NFL journey began as a teenage ball boy with the Denver Broncos during their 1993 training camp. The Colorado native served an internship with that club in 2005 before making assistant coaching stops in Houston, Washington, Cleveland and Atlanta. McDaniel oversaw the San Francisco 49ers' attack in 2021 before taking charge of the Miami Dolphins in 2022. The one-of-a-kind Yale graduate is considered one of the NFL's finest attacking minds and said: 'I knew very early on that I didn't totally look the part, so I'd better be able to help a player or two with my knowledge.'

TYREEK HILL – WIDE RECEIVER

Despite a weaker year, by his high standards, in 2024, Tyreek Hill still strikes fear into opposing defenses and remains as blisteringly explosive as when he made his NFL debut in 2016. The 31-year-old has been tracked running at more than 23 miles per hour during games, making him one of the fastest players the league has ever seen. Hill spent his first six years with the Kansas City Chiefs, winning a Super Bowl during the 2019 season. The eight-time all-star joined the Dolphins in 2022 and registered more than 1,700 receiving yards in each of his first two campaigns in South Florida (the benchmark for a good wide receiver season is 1,000 yards). Hill – who dipped below that mark for the first time in five seasons in 2024 – is more than just a speedster. While not the biggest of receivers at 5-foot-10 and 191 pounds, Hill is a feisty competitor who can out-jump defenders much bigger than him and come down with the ball. That makes him a complete player and one of the most dangerous threats in the game.

DAN MARINO – QUARTERBACK

Blessed with a rocket of an arm and a lightning-quick release, which meant the ball would come out a split-second after he decided where to send it, Dan Marino was arguably the best pure passer in NFL history and one of the game's greatest quarterbacks. The Pittsburgh native was Miami's first-round draft pick in 1983 and became the league's first 5,000-yard passer in a 1984 campaign that saw the Dolphins lose to San Francisco in Super Bowl 19. It was to be Marino's only visit to the big game. After posting groundbreaking quarterback numbers in an era when defenders could be more physical with offensive players, the electrifying Marino proved to be ahead of his time. When asked how many yards he would throw for in a season today, he answered: 'Probably 7,000 yards.' Marino spent his entire career with the Dolphins, retiring in 1999 as the owner of every passing record in the book. Marino made Miami perennial playoff contenders and was inducted into the Hall of Fame in 2005. He said: 'I think how fortunate I was to play for the Dolphins for 17 years. It's awesome to be in the Hall of Fame and it was awesome to be a Miami Dolphin.'

THE PERFECT SEASON

The Miami Dolphins remain the only NFL team to register a perfect season, winning all 17 games in 1972. Led by legendary coach Don Shula, the Dolphins were a physical team featuring a trio of hard-hitting running backs in Larry Csonka, Mercury Morris and Jim Kiick, as well as a stingy defense. Those strengths helped when backup Earl Morrall subbed for injured quarterback Bob Griese, who broke his ankle in Week 5 and did not return for 11 weeks. The Dolphins won 14 regular season contests before seeing off the Cleveland Browns and Pittsburgh Steelers in the first two rounds of the playoffs. In Super Bowl 7, Miami's defense was in dominant form, meaning first half touchdowns from receiver Howard Twilley and Kiick were enough for a 14-7 win over Washington. Every year, members of the 1972 Dolphins gather to celebrate the last undefeated team falling. A few modern-era teams have come close to matching Miami's historic achievement. The 1984 San Francisco 49ers lost just once, as did the 1985 Chicago Bears (with their defeat coming against the Dolphins), and, in 2007, the New England Patriots won 16 regular season games and two playoff contests before losing to the New York Giants in Super Bowl 42.

★ DID YOU KNOW? ★

For 26 seasons, from 1970 to 1995, Miami were led by Don Shula, who holds the NFL record for most head coach wins with 347. A former NFL defensive back in the 1950s, Shula won a Super Bowl with the Baltimore Colts as a coach in 1968 and twice with the Dolphins in 1972 and 1973.

NEW ENGLAND PATRIOTS

FIRST SEASON
1960

DIVISION
AFC East

COLOURS
Nautical blue, red, new century silver and white

OWNER
Robert Kraft

HEAD COACH
Mike Vrabel

STADIUM
Gillette Stadium (64,628)

NFL TITLES/SUPER BOWLS:
6 (2001, 2003, 2004, 2014, 2016, 2018)

INTRODUCING THE PATRIOTS . . .

Formed as the Boston Patriots in the American Football League in 1960, the New England Patriots did not take on their current name until 1971 – a year after joining the NFL. It is a name that has caused the other 31 NFL teams a fearful shudder for many a season.

While their powers have faded in recent years – a period featuring the departure of the greatest double act in NFL history in quarterback Tom Brady and head coach Bill Belichick – memories of New England's dominance over the rest of the league remain fresh.

The Patriots reached Super Bowls in 1985 and 1996 but were comfortably beaten by the Chicago Bears and Green Bay Packers respectively. However, their fortunes improved massively once Belichick arrived in 2000 and the little-known Brady emerged as a star in 2001.

New England won their first title in that season and proceeded to dominate the league for almost two decades. Brady delivered further Super Bowl glory in the 2003, 2004, 2014, 2016 and 2018 campaigns. In a 19-season Brady and Belichick-inspired run, from 2001 to 2018, New England reached the playoffs 17 times, clinched the AFC East division on 17 occasions and won a record-tying six of nine Super Bowl appearances.

Brady departed after the 2019 season and then Belichick, following a 2023 struggle in which the Patriots won just four games. Another difficult four-win campaign cost Jerod Mayo his job as head coach in 2024 and any comeback will now be powered by the team's former linebacker, Mike Vrabel, and promising young quarterback Drake Maye, who was chosen in the first round of the 2024 NFL Draft.

HOME

GILLETTE STADIUM

Gillette Stadium has served as the home of the Patriots since 2002 and is also the base for Major League Soccer's New England Revolution. The entrance includes the tallest lighthouse in the United States and a bridge modelled on Boston's Longfellow Bridge. Its curved video board covering 22,000 square feet is the largest in America. Situated 27 miles south of Boston, Gillette Stadium will serve as a venue for the 2026 FIFA World Cup.

HEAD COACH

MIKE VRABEL

The Patriots are led by a familiar face to their fans in Mike Vrabel, who played linebacker in New England from 2001 to 2008, winning three Super Bowls during a spell in which he established himself as one of the greatest players in team history. After retiring in 2010, Vrabel gained valuable coaching experience in the college ranks before becoming linebackers coach of the Houston Texans in 2014. He served as head coach of the Tennessee Titans from 2018 to 2023, building a reputation as a hands-on coach who regularly fielded competitive and well-drilled teams. Vrabel, who was named NFL Coach of the Year in 2021, explained his active on-field approach when he said: 'Being a coach is about helping out wherever you can. There's no job too small if it can help us win. They pay me to coach instead of standing around.' Vrabel was hired by the Patriots in January 2025.

STAR MAN

DRAKE MAYE – QUARTERBACK

It took just 12 starts as a rookie in 2024 for Drake Maye to show that the New England Patriots have likely found their long-term answer at quarterback. Chosen third overall in the 2024 NFL Draft, the strong-armed and athletic Maye played with a fearless, never-backs-down mentality and offered great hope for the future, despite not being surrounded by elite talent. Maye has the physical skills and mental bravery to attack every inch of the field and his star should rise as the Patriots strengthen their roster around him. Los Angeles Rams head coach Sean McVay got a close look at Maye during his team's mid-season win over New England in 2024 and said: 'He looks like a stud. You can just see the impact that he has on his teammates, the way people talk about him here. He looks like he's going to be a special player for a long time.'

TOM BRADY – QUARTERBACK

Tom Brady went from humble beginnings as the 199th player selected in the 2000 NFL Draft to the greatest player in league history, as a quarterback who won more Super Bowls than any other individual or team, with seven! The sixth-round pick out of Michigan attempted just three passes as an overlooked rookie. But when starter Drew Bledsoe was lost to a season-ending chest injury in 2001, Brady led New England to a first Super Bowl win. He never looked back. Brady guided the Patriots to nine Super Bowl visits, winning the title game on six occasions. The California native had the physical tools to make every throw in the book, but what separated him was his football intelligence, his ability to deliver in the biggest moments and a fierce determination to win year after year. The five-time Super Bowl Most Valuable Player and three-time NFL MVP said: 'Once you experience the winning, that's really the only thing that matters.' Brady proved to be the ultimate winner after he left New England, immediately guiding a Tampa Bay Buccaneers team coming off three straight losing campaigns to Super Bowl success in the 2020 season. No wonder Brady is hailed as The GOAT (Greatest Of All Time).

BRADY'S FINEST HOUR

In Super Bowl 51 at the end of the 2016 season, Tom Brady showed all of his class and greatness in leading New England to victory over the Atlanta Falcons. It was a win that required every ounce of Brady's skill, courage and determination. Atlanta led 21-3 at halftime, having scored three touchdowns, including an interception return of Brady. Things got worse midway through the third period as the Falcons stretched into a 28-3 lead. Brady was immediately off the bench, screaming at his teammates: 'Let's start showing some fight now. We've got to give it all we've got.' While New England's heads were down, wide receiver Julian Edelman believed, as he said: 'Let's go, boys. It's going to be one hell of a story.' Brady got red-hot during a remarkable comeback, throwing touchdown passes to James White and Danny Amendola before White scored on a one-yard run with 57 seconds remaining. The Patriots still trailed 28-26, but tied the game on Brady's two-point conversion pass to Amendola. The first Super Bowl to go into overtime was quickly decided on the opening drive of the extra period. Brady took New England downfield, capping an improbable win on White's two-yard run.

★ DID YOU KNOW? ★

Englishman John Smith kicked for the Patriots from 1974 to 1983, having given up a career in teaching in the UK to attend a tryout with the team. The Oxfordshire native twice led the NFL in scoring and earned all-star honours in 1980. After his playing career, Smith co-presented the early NFL television coverage in the UK on Channel 4.

NEW YORK JETS

FIRST SEASON
1960

DIVISION
AFC East

COLOURS
Gotham green, stealth black and spotlight white

OWNER
Woody and Christopher Johnson

HEAD COACH
Aaron Glenn

STADIUM
MetLife Stadium (82,500)

NFL TITLES/SUPER BOWLS:
1 (1968)

NEW YORK JETS

INTRODUCING THE JETS . . .

As you would expect for a team playing in the Big Apple, the New York Jets get a lot of attention in NFL circles. But the spotlight has not been kind to this squad or New York's passionate fans.

Struggling to find consistency and star power on the offensive side of the ball in particular, the Jets have missed the playoffs in each of the past 14 seasons. Their last serious runs at Super Bowl glory came in the 2009 and 2010 campaigns. They reached the AFC Championship Game on both occasions before falling to the Indianapolis Colts and Pittsburgh Steelers respectively.

New York's lone title success came in Super Bowl 3 at the end of the 1968 season. So, it's been a while! The Jets are embarking on another new era in 2025 as former cornerback Aaron Glenn returns to lead his old team.

Glenn's area of expertise is on the defensive side of the ball and he is the head coach of a team with one of the best defenses in the NFL. That unit is led by the playmaking duo of edge rusher Will McDonald IV and cornerback Ahmad 'Sauce' Gardner.

After two unsuccessful seasons with future Hall of Famer Aaron Rodgers at the helm, New York's attack will now be led by former first-round quarterback Justin Fields, who has previously played for the Chicago Bears and Pittsburgh Steelers. The athletic Fields – who is one of the best running quarterbacks in the league – is supported by wide receiver Garrett Wilson and running back Breece Hall.

Fields has endured a bumpy time since entering the NFL in 2021, much like the team he now leads! Jets fans will be hoping their newest arrival can spark a run to the playoffs for the first time since the 2010 season.

HOME

MetLife STADIUM
The Jets play five miles west of New York City at MetLife Stadium. The open-air, multi-purpose venue cost $1.6 billion and opened in 2010. At its completion, it was the most expensive stadium built in the United States. The 82,500-seat venue hosted Super Bowl 48 at the end of the 2013 season and is scheduled to host the FIFA World Cup final in 2026. MetLife Stadium is also home to the New York Giants – luckily, they are never scheduled to play home games on the same day.

HEAD COACH

AARON GLENN
New York's head coach, Aaron Glenn, is a former cornerback who played for the team from 1994 to 2001. The 53-year-old recorded 634 tackles and 41 interceptions in a 15-year playing career that also saw him suit up for the Houston Texans, Dallas Cowboys, Jacksonville Jaguars and New Orleans Saints. The three-time all-star retired in 2008 and began his coaching career as an assistant with the Cleveland Browns in 2014. After five subsequent seasons with the Saints, he joined the Detroit Lions in 2021 and served as their defensive coordinator for four campaigns before being taking charge of the Jets in January 2025. As a former player, Glenn has a great connection with his team. But he can also get tough, as he showed early in the 2025 offseason by moving on from a Hall of Fame-level quarterback in Aaron Rodgers.

AHMAD 'SAUCE' GARDNER – CORNERBACK

The Jets have arguably the best cornerback in the NFL – and one of the very best defenders in the league – on their roster in the form of Ahmad 'Sauce' Gardner. That nickname was given to Gardner when he was growing up in Detroit, Michigan, as the two-time Pro Bowl all-star explained: 'My Little League coach gave me that name because of the swagger I had. It still fits me perfectly.' Gardner has not lacked confidence since entering the NFL as a first-round pick for the Jets in 2022. The 25-year-old has the speed and change-of-direction skills to mirror the fastest receivers in the game. But his size is an added weapon. At 6-foot-3 and 190 pounds, Gardner is one of the biggest cornerbacks in the NFL and one who is capable of going toe to toe with physical wide receivers. Gardner is a reminder that statistics can often be misleading. He has had just three interceptions in his first three NFL seasons to date. But that should not be an indictment on his skills. It's a reminder that opposing quarterbacks are rarely confident attacking his area of the field due to his elite coverage ability.

JOE NAMATH – QUARTERBACK

It takes a big character to succeed as a quarterback in New York and that was never an issue for 'Broadway' Joe Namath, who shone as bright as the city's lights from 1965 to 1976. During the 1960s, the NFL was in a player bidding war with the rival American Football League (the two merged in 1970). After starring at the University of Alabama, Namath was a first-round pick in both leagues in 1965. He was chosen by the NFL's St. Louis Cardinals and by the AFL's Jets, who dangled a then-record contract worth $427,000. Namath chose the Jets and proved worthy of that hefty investment. At a time when teams preferred to run the ball, Namath was a trailblazer who attacked through the air. The five-time all-star was pro football's first 4,000-yard passer in 1967. A season later, the Hall of Famer delivered the Jets' only Super Bowl crown.

THE GUARANTEE

Joe Namath was never short of confidence during his outstanding 12-year spell with the New York Jets. How else could you explain the quarterback donning ladies' tights in a famous advertising campaign in the 1960s? But perhaps his most overt and legendary display of confidence came in Miami ahead of Super Bowl 3 against the Baltimore Colts. Just days before taking on what was being hailed as 'the great football team in history', Namath delivered 'The Guarantee'. After being heckled at an awards dinner, he said: 'We're going to win the game. I guarantee it.' Established football minds looked down their noses at the American Football League at that time. A situation not helped by the NFL's Green Bay Packers easily winning the first two Super Bowls pitting each league's champions against each other. Namath couldn't have cared less. The Jets ignored their status as massive underdogs and shocked the sports world with a 16-7 win. Their quarterback was named the game's Most Valuable Player and the sight of Namath pointing to the sky as he jogged from the field after the upset win remains iconic. Namath not only delivered a victory for the Jets, he gave legitimacy to an entire league.

★ DID YOU KNOW? ★

While their first season was in 1960, the New York Jets did not play under the name we know today until the 1963 campaign. Founded in 1959, they were originally known as The Titans of New York and played at the Polo Grounds – a dual-purpose baseball and American football stadium in upper Manhattan.

PITTSBURGH STEELERS

FIRST SEASON
1933

DIVISION
AFC North

COLOURS
Black and gold

OWNER
The Rooney Family

HEAD COACH
Mike Tomlin

STADIUM
Acrisure Stadium (68,400)

NFL TITLES/SUPER BOWLS:
6 (1974, 1975, 1978, 1979, 2005, 2008)

PITTSBURGH STEELERS

INTRODUCING THE STEELERS . . .

Very few NFL teams can boast a history and tradition as rich as that of the Pittsburgh Steelers, who are one of the league's most iconic teams. Formed in 1933, the Steelers have produced some of the NFL's biggest superstars over the decades and those players are beloved in the city of Pittsburgh.

The bond between Steelers players and their fans, who wave bright yellow 'Terrible Towels' on gamedays, is an unbreakable one. And there has been plenty for all who love the Steelers to celebrate. A dominance of the 1970s saw the Steelers win four NFL crowns in six seasons (1974, 1975, 1978 and 1979). They added Vince Lombardi Trophies in the 2005 and 2008 campaigns, bringing their total of Super Bowl wins to a record-tying six.

The fruits of those labours are proudly displayed at the team's headquarters, and they serve a purpose every day, as inspirational head coach Mike Tomlin explained: 'Nothing needs to be said to the players when they walk past those Lombardi Trophies – it's a reminder of what we're doing here and not a subtle one.'

Having reached the AFC playoffs eight times since 2014, the Steelers are not merely living in the past, but they do give a respectful nod to their history and to what has become known as 'The Standard'. Tomlin said: 'History is the ultimate motivator for us. The standard has been set here long before myself and these young men. It's our job to adhere to that. Our goals are simple – we need to put ourselves in the position to be in the tournament, compete for that world championship and to win it. That will be our goal every year.'

HOME

ACRISURE STADIUM

With its bright yellow seats that are open to the Pennsylvania elements, passionate fans, and tremendous views of downtown Pittsburgh and the confluence of the Allegheny, Monongahela and Ohio Rivers, a visit to Acrisure Stadium should be on the wish-list of every NFL fan. The venue, which opened in 2001, rocks with emotion at the start of every fourth quarter when the Styx song 'Renegade' is blasted to fire up the home team and its fans.

HEAD COACH

MIKE TOMLIN

The Steelers are loyal when it comes to their head coaches, hiring only three in more than half a century in Chuck Noll, Bill Cowher and Mike Tomlin, who joined Pittsburgh in 2007. But that loyalty has never been misplaced, as all three delivered Super Bowl success. Tomlin – a self-described 'highly compensated P.E. teacher' – was the youngest head coach in the NFL when hired at the age of 34. He won a Super Bowl at 36. While his expertise lies on the defensive side of the ball, Tomlin's strongest skill is his ability to lead and inspire his players as one of the NFL's greatest motivators. The 2024 season marked the 18th campaign in a row where Tomlin has avoided a losing record – a historic milestone for a head coach.

T.J. WATT – OUTSIDE LINEBACKER/EDGE RUSHER

Pittsburgh's dominance in the 1970s was powered by one of the greatest defenses in NFL history – a unit feared around the league, which was known as 'The Steel Curtain'. That group was as intimidating as it was talented. And they set a benchmark and paved the way for many great defensive players to shine for the Steelers in the ensuing decades. So, it's fitting that the best player on the team today is a defender who also happens to be one of the NFL's elite superstars. Outside linebacker/edge rusher T.J. Watt is a skilled, energetic and relentless player who has proven to be a nightmare for opposing quarterbacks in his eight NFL seasons to date. Watt won NFL Defensive Player of the Year honours in 2021 when tying the league's single-season sacks record with 22½. The seven-time all-star registered 88 sacks in his first 100 NFL games, ranking second in NFL history as he moved past elder brother J.J., who was a three-time NFL Defensive Player of the Year with the Houston Texans. T.J.'s greatest skill cannot be measured in mere statistics and awards, however – when the Steelers need an emotional lift, the 30-year-old always seems to deliver.

'MEAN' JOE GREENE – DEFENSIVE END

The Steelers were a downtrodden franchise heading into the 1969 NFL Draft, having posted a losing record in each of the previous five seasons. But by adding North Texas State defensive tackle 'Mean' Joe Greene in the first round, Pittsburgh changed their fortunes in an instant. Greene was the rock upon which Pittsburgh's dominant 'Steel Curtain' defense was built. That unit featured some of the sport's most intimidating hitters in toothless linebacker Jack Lambert and cornerback Mel Blount. But Greene was the greatest of a historic bunch and is celebrated as the best player in team history. With Greene throwing massive offensive linemen around like they were small children and demanding the same level of intensity from his teammates, the Steelers won four Super Bowls and their star man was a two-time NFL Defensive Player of the Year and a 10-time all-star. Greene is forever immortalised in the Pro Football Hall of Fame.

THE IMMACULATE RECEPTION

During the 1972 AFC playoffs, the Steelers trailed the Oakland Raiders 7-6 with 22 seconds remaining. Steelers Hall of Fame quarterback Terry Bradshaw faced a fourth-and-10 from his own 40-yard line. Failure would be season-ending. Bradshaw threw a desperation pass to Frenchy Fuqua and the running back was immediately hit by Raiders safety Jack Tatum, catapulting the ball back towards the Pittsburgh end of the field. Steelers' Hall of Fame running back Franco Harris was trailing the play and couldn't believe his luck as he scooped the ball off his shoelaces and sprinted for a miraculous game-winning score. Jubilant fans stormed the field, delaying the conversion attempt by 15 minutes. It was enough time for referee Fred Swearingen to determine the legality of the play. If the ball had bounced off Fuqua without touching Tatum, the catch would have been ruled illegal. If the ball touched only Tatum, or Tatum and Fuqua, it would be legal. It was VAR drama in the 1970s! The touchdown ruling stood and Pittsburgh won 13-7. The Immaculate Reception is often pointed to as the moment the Steelers' dynasty was born.

★ DID YOU KNOW? ★

The Terrible Towel was the brainchild of Steelers radio broadcaster Myron Cope. He was asked by his bosses at WTAE to fire up the crowd ahead of Pittsburgh's playoff contest against the Baltimore Colts on 27 December 1975. Fans waved yellow towels and dishcloths throughout a 28-10 win and the legend of the Terrible Towel was born. Terrible Towels have made their way to the top of Mount Everest and onto the International Space Station.

TENNESSEE TITANS

FIRST SEASON
1960

DIVISION
AFC South

COLOURS
Navy, Titans blue, red, silver and white

OWNER
Amy Adams Strunk

HEAD COACH
Brian Callahan

STADIUM
Nissan Stadium (69,143)

NFL TITLES/SUPER BOWLS:
0

TENNESSEE TITANS

INTRODUCING THE TITANS . . .

The Titans were founded under a different name and in a different city, beginning play in the American Football League as the Houston Oilers in 1960. Formed by Houston-based oil tycoon Bud Adams, the Oilers won the first two AFL championships before moving to the NFL in 1970.

When in Houston, the Oilers fielded some legendary players, including running back Earl Campbell and a fellow Hall of Famer in quarterback Warren Moon. The team was beloved by the fans in Texas, but Adams re-located the franchise to Nashville, Tennessee, in 1997.

After playing two seasons as the Tennessee Oilers, the team became known as the Titans in 1999 and reached Super Bowl 34 against the St. Louis Rams. Looking to tie the score on the game's final play, wide receiver Kevin Dyson was famously tackled just one yard short of a touchdown by Mike Jones. It was a heartbreaking loss, as the Titans have never made it back to the big game. Losing at the Super Bowl semi-final stage in the 2002 and 2019 seasons is the closest they have come.

Titans teams have traditionally been tough and competitive, but the current squad is looking to rebuild. After making the playoffs for three years in a row, from 2019 to 2021, Tennessee have now failed to qualify for the season's knockout stages in each of the past three campaigns.

With one of the NFL's better defenses already in place, the emphasis is on finding offensive talent similar to some of the greats who have donned a Titans uniform in the past. That quest started with the selection of quarterback Cam Ward with the first pick in the 2025 NFL Draft.

HOME

NISSAN STADIUM

The Titans began playing in Nissan Stadium in 1999. Located on the east bank of Nashville's Cumberland River, the 69,143-seat venue has also hosted NHL ice hockey games, the Monster Jam World Finals and soccer matches for the US men's and women's teams, as well as a host of music concerts, including The Rolling Stones, Ed Sheeran and One Direction.

HEAD COACH

BRIAN CALLAHAN

Upon being hired by the Titans in 2024, head coach Brian Callahan revealed that he was inspired during his rise up the NFL ranks by the leadership of then-Liverpool F.C. boss Jurgen Klopp. The pair even spoke on Zoom shortly after Callahan's appointment. The son of former NFL head coach Bill Callahan (Las Vegas Raiders), Brian got his first NFL break as an assistant with Denver in 2010. After further stops with Detroit, the Raiders and Cincinnati, where he ran their attack for five seasons, the junior Callahan landed with Tennessee and immediately hired his father to be his offensive line coach.

STAR MAN

JEFFERY SIMMONS – DEFENSIVE TACKLE

The beating heart of the Tennessee Titans defense plays right in the middle of their defensive line and is a dominant force by the name of Jeffery Simmons. The three-time all-star, who entered the NFL as a first-round pick in 2019, is strong (he has been known to shove elite 320-pound offensive linemen to the floor with just one arm) and explosive, making him a force against running and passing plays. That skillset makes Simmons hard to neutralise on Sundays – if you try to beat him with power, you'd better bring two blockers, and you will still need to hope for some luck. And if you try to match his intensity and athleticism, there are very few offensive linemen who can move like him. So, on most occasions, Simmons is going to be a problem. Simmons is also a talker on the field, before kick-off, when he routinely hypes up his teammates, and throughout each contest, intimidating those who line up against him. Pittsburgh Steelers running back Jaylen Warren told NFL Films: 'He's the guy on their defense that gets them going. He is the kingpin of their defense. He's out there fighting each and every play, giving all that he's got.'

EARL CAMPBELL – RUNNING BACK

The Titans have rolled out a procession of powerful running backs throughout their history. Before the great Derrick Henry (2016–2023), there was Eddie George (1996–2003), and before him was arguably the greatest player in franchise history in Earl Campbell, who starred in Houston from 1978 to 1984. Campbell had a relatively short career, retiring in 1985 after a season and a half with the New Orleans Saints, but his impact on the league and on those who tried to tackle him was historic. The Hall of Famer was a physically imposing force who pounded the heart of a defense before sprinting away from those he was choosing to run over just moments earlier. Former Detroit Lions linebacker Ed O'Neil said: 'Earl Campbell was ridiculous. He was so strong and powerful and he just wanted to run over everybody.' Tales of Campbell's strength became the stuff of legend before he even entered the NFL. While playing college football at the University of Texas, Campbell sprinted into the end zone to score and knocked over the Houston Cougars' team mascot in the process. But this was not a person in a furry suit and over-sized head – the mascot was a fully-grown longhorn cow named Bevo, who thankfully returned to his feet unharmed!

THE MUSIC CITY MIRACLE

The most celebrated play in Titans history was originally labelled 'Home Run Throwback' by then-head coach Jeff Fisher and special teams coach Alan Lowry. But as is often the case with incredible plays that become iconic, it needed a catchy nickname and will forever be known as 'The Music City Miracle'. The Titans trailed Buffalo 16-15 with 16 seconds remaining in the first round of the 1999 season's playoffs. The Bills kicked off after seemingly snatching victory through Steve Christie's field goal. The ball was fielded by fullback Lorenzo Neal, who handed it to Frank Wycheck. The tight end took a few steps to his right and then threw from the 25-yard line across the field to wide receiver Kevin Dyson, who worked behind a wall of blockers before sprinting down the left sideline for a 75-yard touchdown. The drama was dragged out as officials assessed whether Wycheck's cross-field lateral had, in fact, illegally travelled forwards – teams can pass backwards as many times as they like, but can only pass forwards once per play on scrimmage plays and never on a kick-off return. It was close. And you will still find Buffalo fans to this day who insist it was a forward pass. Referee Phil Luckett stared into the replay monitor for what seemed like an eternity before jogging onto the field to announce: 'The ruling stands . . . it was a lateral . . . touchdown.'

★ DID YOU KNOW? ★

When the Minnesota Vikings completed a comeback from 33-0 down to beat the Indianapolis Colts 39-36 in December 2022, it erased a black mark from Titans' history. With the team known as the Houston Oilers at the time, the 1992 season's playoffs saw Buffalo come back from 35-3 down to tie the game at 35-35 and eventually win 41-38 in overtime. Houston owned the largest blown lead in NFL history for more than 30 years before the Colts took the unwanted honour.

The National Football Conference (NFC)

The National Football Conference (NFC) is heavily comprised of teams who were playing in the NFL before the league merged with the AFL in 1970. Teams that were around at the time the NFL launched in 1920 include founder members in the Arizona Cardinals and Chicago Bears, as well as the Green Bay Packers.

Some of the league's oldest and most storied franchises reside in the NFC, with the New York Giants, Detroit Lions, Washington Commanders, Philadelphia Eagles and Los Angeles Rams having been in existence since at least the 1937 season. The conference has also been home to some of the most powerful dynasties the league has ever seen in the form of the 1960s Packers, the 1980s San Francisco 49ers and the Dallas Cowboys of the 1990s.

While Super Bowl success has been split fairly evenly across the AFC and NFC in recent years, there was a dominant period when the National Conference was top dog. From 1984 to 1996, teams from the NFC won 13 Super Bowls in a row. Those wins played into a long-held belief that the tougher and more physical teams in the NFL were in the NFC, while the flashier, pass-happy clubs played in the AFC.

Where the Chiefs and Patriots have dominated the AFC in recent times, success has been more fleeting and spread around in the NFC. Over the past 15 seasons, nine different teams have reached the Super Bowl, including the reigning 2024 champions, the Philadelphia Eagles.

ARIZONA CARDINALS

FIRST SEASON
1898

DIVISION
NFC West

COLOURS
Cardinal red, black and white

OWNER
Michael Bidwill

HEAD COACH
Jonathan Gannon

STADIUM
State Farm Stadium (65,000)

NFL TITLES/SUPER BOWLS:
2 (1925, 1947)

ARIZONA CARDINALS

INTRODUCING THE CARDINALS . . .

Founded as the Morgan Athletic Club in 1898 – long before the NFL was born in 1920 – the Cardinals are the oldest continuously run professional American football team in the world. Along with the Chicago Bears, the Cardinals are the only other current club that played in the league's inaugural season.

The Cardinals were based in Chicago from 1920 to 1943, and again after World War II from 1945 to 1959. They played the 1944 season as Card-Pitt, a combination of athletes from the Cardinals and Pittsburgh Steelers, as the league coped with a player shortage due to the war. They became the St. Louis Cardinals after moving to that city in 1960 and stayed there until 1987. A move to the desert saw them become the Phoenix Cardinals in 1988, and they changed to their current name, the Arizona Cardinals, in 1994.

All those iterations of the Cardinals have produced two championships (in 1925 and 1947), but the franchise has never won a Super Bowl. Their only appearance in the big game came during the 2008 season, when they were powered by NFL Most Valuable Player quarterback Kurt Warner. Arizona were huge underdogs against the Steelers but led 23-20 inside the game's final minute. They were beaten by Santonio Holmes' spectacular touchdown catch with just 35 seconds remaining.

Arizona's last serious Super Bowl challenge came in 2015, when they made it all the way to the NFC Championship Game before losing to the Carolina Panthers. The modern-day Cardinals have missed the playoffs eight out of nine times since 2016, but harbour hopes of a competitive future led by playmaking quarterback Kyler Murray and exciting young wide receiver Marvin Harrison Jr.

HOME

STATE FARM STADIUM

The Cardinals' home features a retractable roof that can be opened on cooler days in the Arizona desert, but when closed it means the team can play in air-conditioned comfort. A necessity early in the NFL season. The 65,000-seat venue opened in 2006 and has hosted three Super Bowls, in the 2007, 2014 and 2022 seasons. The grass field can be rolled out of the stadium to allow natural sunlight to reach the playing surface.

HEAD COACH

JONATHAN GANNON

The Cardinals are led by a coach whose expertise came on defense. Jonathan Gannon was a wide receiver and defensive back in high school, but he suffered a career-ending injury when at the University of Louisville. During his remaining time at the school, Gannon served as an assistant coach before entering the NFL with the Atlanta Falcons in 2007. He also coached with Tennessee, Minnesota and Indianapolis before leading the Philadelphia Eagles' defense in 2021 and 2022. After losing Super Bowl 57 with the Eagles in Arizona's stadium, he was named the Cardinals' head coach two days later on 14 February 2023.

KYLER MURRAY – QUARTERBACK

Arizona's attack is led by a star who constantly frustrates opposing defenses in quarterback Kyler Murray. The 2019 NFL Draft's first pick epitomises the league's new approach to his position. Quarterbacks no longer have to be 6-foot-5, solely standing behind their line making throws. They can come in any shape and size if they are athletic and can still make the necessary passes downfield. Murray does it all, despite being one of the shortest quarterbacks in the game at 5-foot-10. The two-time all-star sprints around like he is in a video game and then throws to attack often-exhausted defensive backs. Murray strikes fear into the hearts of most Arizona opponents and is always the Cardinals' number-one player to stop. New York Jets cornerback Isaiah Oliver explains: 'You have to prepare for him specifically, otherwise it can get bad for you. He is that special with how he can create plays outside of the pocket and on designed quarterback runs. There are endless amounts of things he can do.' Murray's skills do not end with American football – he was chosen ninth overall by Major League Baseball's Oakland Athletics in their 2018 Draft, but opted for a career in the NFL.

LARRY FITZGERALD – WIDE RECEIVER

You may reply by shouting 'that's what he is supposed to do', but Arizona's Larry Fitzgerald was really good at catching the football when he starred for the Cardinals for 17 seasons from 2004 to 2020. Fitzgerald caught 1,378 passes and registered just 29 drops. An incredible feat. The son of NFL reporter Larry Fitzgerald Sr. was the model of consistency on and off the field and, by the time he retired, the 11-time all-star was the proud owner of 40 team records and several league marks, including registering eight seasons with at least 90 catches. Fitzgerald was never the fastest, but he played with great technique and precision and benefited from learning at a young age what it would take to succeed in the NFL. Fitzgerald served as a training camp ball boy with the Minnesota Vikings and closely watched legendary receivers such as Cris Carter and Randy Moss, explaining: 'I was about seven or eight years old and that really helped me. I saw their work ethic – I saw the way they practised, the way they took care of their bodies, the way they ate, the way they trained. I saw that if I wanted to be great, these were some of the things I had to do.'

WARNER'S MAGICAL NIGHT

The Cardinals featured in the highest-scoring playoff game in NFL history during the 2009 season, as they recorded a spectacular 51-45 victory over the Green Bay Packers. Hall of Fame quarterback Kurt Warner was in the form of his life as he threw more touchdown passes (five) than incompletions (four). In the final home game of his career, Warner hit on 29 of 33 passes for 379 yards and did not throw an interception. Green Bay quarterback Aaron Rodgers – a sure-fire Hall of Famer himself when he retires – was almost as effective as he threw for 423 yards and four touchdowns. There was late drama as Arizona's Neil Rackers missed an easy 34-yard field goal with 14 seconds remaining, sending the teams into sudden-death overtime tied at 45-45. On the first drive of the extra period, a game dominated by both attacks was decided on defense as Michael Adams sacked Rodgers, popping the ball into the air. Linebacker Karlos Dansby grabbed it and rumbled 17 yards to the end zone for the winning touchdown, sparking wild scenes of celebration in Arizona.

★ DID YOU KNOW? ★

Kurt Warner – who played for the Cardinals from 2005 to 2009 – gained valuable experience by playing in NFL Europe (a developmental league that operated in Europe from 1991–1992 and again from 1995–2007) with the Amsterdam Admirals in 1998. Warner went on to the NFL, where he would win two NFL MVP awards and a Super Bowl MVP prize after leading the St. Louis Rams to glory during the 1999 season.

ATLANTA FALCONS

FIRST SEASON
1966

OWNER
Arthur Blank

DIVISION
NFC South

HEAD COACH
Raheem Morris

COLOURS
Black, red, silver and white

STADIUM
Mercedes-Benz Stadium (71,000)

NFL TITLES/SUPER BOWLS:
0

ATLANTA FALCONS

INTRODUCING THE FALCONS . . .

The Atlanta Falcons have routinely fielded some of the most exciting players of their generation – talents such as cornerback and return sensation Deion 'Prime Time' Sanders, quarterback Matt Ryan, tight end Tony Gonzalez and wide receiver Julio Jones. But they are still awaiting their first Super Bowl success.

The team that proudly uses the 'Rise Up' slogan has done so in notable fashion throughout their history. The Falcons were born in 1966 but did not truly take flight until their first playoff season of 1978. They reached and lost Super Bowls in the 1998 and 2016 seasons to the Denver Broncos and New England Patriots respectively. That loss to New England in Super Bowl 51 was especially painful, as the Falcons led 28-3 midway through the third quarter before falling to an infamous, heartbreaking 34-28 defeat in overtime. Atlanta have come close on other occasions, losing NFC Championship Games to the Philadelphia Eagles in 2004 and the San Francisco 49ers in 2012.

Atlanta have failed to make the playoffs in each of the past seven seasons. Any change in fortune will be led by explosive and game-breaking quarterback Michael Penix Jr., who was chosen in the first round of the 2024 NFL Draft. His selection was somewhat of a surprise considering the financial investment that had already been made in $100 million veteran quarterback Kirk Cousins, but, by the end of 2024, it was Penix at the helm of an intriguing attack that features dynamic running back Bijan Robinson and passing game playmakers in receivers Drake London and Darnell Mooney, and tight end Kyle Pitts.

HOME

MERCEDES-BENZ STADIUM

The Falcons play at the impressive Mercedes-Benz Stadium, which opened in 2017. Games can be played indoors and outdoors as the 71,000-seat venue features a retractable roof that opens in 12 minutes. The stadium – which is also home to Major League Soccer's Atlanta United F.C. – hosted Super Bowl 53 at the end of the 2018 season and will showcase eight games at the 2026 FIFA World Cup, including one semi-final. The stadium will host Super Bowl 62 to cap the 2027 season.

HEAD COACH

RAHEEM MORRIS

Raheem Morris is in his second stint as a full-time head coach, having been appointed by Atlanta in 2024. Morris led the Tampa Bay Buccaneers from 2009 to 2011. Either side of that, he won Super Bowls as an assistant with the Buccaneers in 2002 and with the Los Angeles Rams in 2021. Morris also served as interim head coach of the Falcons in 2020 following the firing of Dan Quinn, leading Atlanta to all four of their wins that season. The 49-year-old's background is on defense, but Morris is also a great communicator who is popular with all players. Morris explained his coaching style when he said: 'I really believe you've got to be a good listener, first with the players, and then you can actually go out there and execute whatever you want to get done. And once they know you care about them, they're willing to do whatever they want to do for you.'

BIJAN ROBINSON – RUNNING BACK

Atlanta's attack is built around one of the best and most elusive running backs in the NFL today in Bijan Robinson. The first-round pick from the University of Texas in 2023 is as polite, humble and likeable off the field as he is talented and dangerous on the gridiron. Robinson said: 'I feel it's always great to have the best character you can have because you play a game where a lot of people see you play. After games, you get to have a platform to speak and let those people hear you. And you want those little kids and those teenagers or adults to be like, "Man, I can really relate to this dude." ' The only people who probably don't like Robinson are the NFL defenders he embarrasses on Sundays. Growing up as a huge fan of Detroit Lions legend Barry Sanders, Robinson consistently emulates the moves of his heroes, spinning, ducking and dodging away from would-be tacklers before sprinting downfield. Robinson proved his importance to the Falcons throughout a 2024 season in which he racked up 1,887 combined yards rushing and receiving – ranking him fourth in the league. This all-round star is set to dominate the NFL for years to come.

MATT RYAN – QUARTERBACK

Having been chosen third overall by the Falcons in the 2008 NFL Draft, rookie quarterback Matt Ryan announced his arrival on the NFL stage by throwing a 62-yard touchdown pass to Michael Jenkins on his very first throw. 'It was a good, fast start,' Ryan would later say. Falcons fans had been treated to a preview of what was to come. During 14 seasons in Atlanta, Ryan became the epitome of poise, production and high-level consistency. Football intelligence and accurate passes became the trademark of a four-time Pro Bowler who rarely let his team down. Evidence of his outstanding consistency can be found in the decade from 2011 to 2020, when Ryan unleashed 10 straight seasons with at least 4,000 passing yards. Consistency was not just a buzzword for Ryan, it became his NFL way of life. Ryan explained: 'The biggest thing I've learned during my time in the NFL is that the same guy has to show up every Sunday. You can't do it one week and then do nothing the next.' Ryan's best came in 2016 when he guided the Falcons to Super Bowl 51 and was named the NFL's Most Valuable Player along the way. While many focus on how Atlanta lost that big game, it should not detract from Ryan's outstanding career.

MORTEN TAMES THE VIKINGS

The 1998 NFC Championship Game seemed a mere formality for the Minnesota Vikings – a box to be ticked before advancing to Super Bowl 34. The Vikings had gone 15-1 in the regular season and every other team in NFL history with that record had reached the title game. Led by quarterback Randall Cunningham and featuring Hall of Fame wide receivers Randy Moss and Cris Carter, the Vikings set an NFL record by scoring 556 points in the regular season. And they boasted a kicker in Gary Anderson who had not missed a field goal or an extra point all year. The only problem? Somebody forgot to tell the Atlanta Falcons to roll over and die as they travelled to play the Vikings in Minnesota. The Falcons punched above their weight all night long and quarterback Chris Chandler was outstanding, throwing for 340 yards and three touchdowns. His last touchdown strike to Terance Mathis with 49 seconds remaining sent the game into sudden-death overtime with the score locked at 27-27. And it had come after Anderson handed the Falcons a lifeline by missing an easy 39-yard field goal, which would have given Minnesota a 10-point lead with two minutes remaining. Atlanta's Danish kicker Morten Andersen showed his namesake how it was done in overtime, converting a 38-yard kick to stun the Vikings and send the Falcons to their first Super Bowl.

★ DID YOU KNOW? ★

Mick Luckhurst, who hailed from Redbourn in Hertfordshire, served as kicker of the Atlanta Falcons from 1981 to 1987, successfully converting 115 field goals. In retirement, from 1987 to 1991, Luckhurst became the face of American football coverage in the United Kingdom as the presenter of the action shown each week on Channel 4.

CAROLINA PANTHERS

FIRST SEASON
1995

OWNER
David Tepper

DIVISION
NFC South

HEAD COACH
Dave Canales

COLOURS
Black, process blue, silver

STADIUM
Bank of America Stadium (74,867)

NFL TITLES/SUPER BOWLS:
0

CAROLINA PANTHERS

INTRODUCING THE PANTHERS . . .

The Carolina Panthers have made their presence felt during their relatively brief time in the NFL. After entering the league in 1995 as an expansion franchise, which required a team to be built from scratch with a large percentage of cast-offs from other rosters, the Panthers reached the NFC Championship Game in just their second season.

The Panthers went one step further and qualified for their first Super Bowl during the 2003 campaign, but they were undone by an Adam Vinatieri field goal with four seconds remaining that lifted Tom Brady's New England Patriots to a 32-29 win.

In 2011, the Panthers began to mount another championship challenge through the drafting of dual-threat quarterback Cam Newton. In 2015, Newton was named the NFL's Most Valuable Player as Carolina lost just one game on their way to the 50th Super Bowl. But they lost their second title game, this time by a 24-10 scoreline against the Denver Broncos.

Turbulent times have followed. Carolina have not made the playoffs since the 2017 season and have fired three general managers and three head coaches since 2019. They also traded away three first-round stars in three straight years in running back Christian McCaffrey (2022), wide receiver D.J. Moore (2023) and defensive end Brian Burns (2024).

The rebuild currently underway is not going to be a quick one, but it will rely largely on the relationship between offensive-minded head coach Dave Canales and quarterback Bryce Young – the first player taken in the 2023 NFL Draft. There were signs of hope towards the end of 2024. The Panthers finished the season with five wins and 12 losses, but four of those victories came in the final nine games of the campaign.

BANK OF AMERICA STADIUM

The Panthers play at Bank of America Stadium, which seats 74,867 fans and offers stunning views of downtown Charlotte. Opened in 1996, the venue was dubbed the 'classic American stadium' due to its bowl design. The Panthers plan to make $800 million-worth of renovations to the venue, with work set to begin in 2026.

DAVE CANALES

Twenty years before becoming head coach of the Carolina Panthers, Dave Canales was serving as a high-school coach in California. The former college wide receiver then worked as a video assistant for the University of Southern California's American football team, where he met legendary coach Pete Carroll. Canales worked under Carroll for 13 seasons with the Seattle Seahawks, winning a Super Bowl in the 2013 season. In 2022, Canales oversaw the career resurgence of quarterback Geno Smith. The 44-year-old ran the Tampa Bay Buccaneers' offense in 2023, guiding quarterback Baker Mayfield to a career-defining year, before taking charge of the Panthers in 2024.

CHUBA HUBBARD – RUNNING BACK

The Carolina Panthers are powered by one of the NFL's fast-rising stars in explosive running back Chuba Hubbard. The Canadian, who grew up in Edmonton, Alberta, was drafted as a reserve for star runner Christian McCaffrey in 2021. But Hubbard was thrust into a starting role midway through his rookie season when McCaffrey was traded to San Francisco. And then, in 2023, Hubbard was expected to move into a reserve role behind newly acquired free agent, Miles Sanders, formerly of the Philadelphia Eagles. But that proved to be the other way around and Hubbard is now firmly established as Carolina's best attacking player. European fans got to see Hubbard at his best in Munich, Germany, in 2024. Just days after inking a new four-year deal worth $33 million, Hubbard rushed for a career-high 153 yards and one touchdown in a 20-17 win over the New York Giants. He ended that season breaking the 1,000-yard barrier for the first time with 1,195 rushing yards and 10 touchdowns. Coming from relatively humble beginnings as a fourth-round pick out of Oklahoma State, Hubbard said: 'Your confidence comes from your preparation. One thing I'm always going to do is be prepared. I'm going to keep working hard regardless of my contract or the wins and losses.'

JULIUS PEPPERS – DEFENSIVE END

Julius Peppers was a giant of a player for the Carolina Panthers, in every sense of the word. The 6-foot-7-inch defensive end was the team's second overall pick in the 2002 NFL Draft and became one of the most dominant pass rushers of his era. He played for three teams over a glittering 17-year career and led each of them in sacks at least once (Carolina seven times, Chicago four times, and Green Bay once). A former college basketball star, Peppers played his first eight seasons in Carolina, helping them reach a Super Bowl in 2003, and the final two years of his career with the NFC South club in 2017 and 2018. Even though the Hall of Famer was recognised as the number-one defender to stop each weekend, Peppers still recorded 159½ career sacks and 52 forced fumbles. When he couldn't get to the quarterback, he was just as destructive, recording 11 interceptions and knocking down 79 passes with his long arms. Former NFL head coach Tony Dungy best-epitomised the league-wide respect for the nine-time all-star when he said: 'I just remember the dominance and the physical awesomeness. It just took your breath away. He had that athleticism, that freakish athleticism.'

A DOUBLE OVERTIME CLASSIC

During their march to a first Super Bowl appearance in the 2003 season, the Panthers faced a tricky contest in the second round of the playoffs, travelling to St. Louis to take on the Rams, who had won all eight home games that year. Carolina seemed in good shape to advance as they led 23-12 with just under nine minutes remaining. But the Rams rallied late and sent the game into extra time with the scores tied at 23-23. With the next score winning the contest, the teams played on and on through a fifth quarter. Carolina kicker John Kasay had a successful field goal from 40 yards wiped out as the Panthers were penalised five yards for not snapping the ball before the play clock ran out. He then missed the ensuing kick from 45 yards – the winning points were proving hard to find! On the first play of the sixth period, quarterback Jake Delhomme connected with wide receiver Steve Smith Sr. on a 69-yard touchdown pass that finally catapulted the Panthers to the next round of the playoffs. Incredibly, it was the fourth time the Panthers had won an overtime game during that magical season. Head coach John Fox summed up the feelings of exhausted Carolina fans everywhere when he said: 'I've never seen a game quite like that, let alone be involved in one.'

★ DID YOU KNOW? ★

'Keep pounding' is the rallying cry of the Carolina Panthers. It was the personal motto of the team's linebacker and former assistant coach Sam Mills, who died after a battle with cancer in 2005. Those words are now stitched into the collar of every Panthers jersey. And former players and celebrities are invited to pound a giant drum at Carolina home games, to keep Mills' message alive.

CHICAGO BEARS

FIRST SEASON
1920

DIVISION
NFC North

COLOURS
Navy blue, burnt orange and white

OWNER
George H. McCaskey

HEAD COACH
Ben Johnson

STADIUM
Soldier Field (62,500)

NFL TITLES/SUPER BOWLS:
9 (1921, 1932, 1933, 1940, 1941, 1943, 1946, 1963, 1985)

INTRODUCING THE BEARS . . .

The Chicago Bears boast a legendary history as original members of the National Football League. Their first owner, George 'Papa Bear' Halas, was not only the founder of the Bears, he also formed the league we know and love today back in 1920.

The Bears have won NFL championships in five different decades and only the Green Bay Packers have clinched more league titles (13) than Chicago's nine. But it's now 40 years since the Bears stood proud as NFL champions at the end of an iconic 1985 campaign. The closest they have come since was a 2006 season that saw them lose Super Bowl 41 to the Indianapolis Colts.

The Bears have missed the NFC playoffs each season since 2022, but this current squad offers hope of a competitive future. Many of Chicago's great teams of the past have been built around defensive stars, but the modern-day Bears have the attacking players to win and entertain at the same time.

Quarterback Caleb Williams has already been compared to greats such as Patrick Mahomes and Aaron Rodgers, and the dynamic playmaker boasts exciting weapons in wide receivers D.J. Moore and Rome Odunze, running back D'Andre Swift, and tight end Cole Kmet. After being sacked an NFL-high 68 times as a rookie in 2024, Williams will now work behind a strong and upgraded offensive line in the coming years.

The Bears are a well-supported team and their players recognise the passion of the fans and the expectation levels, as all-star cornerback Jaylon Johnson explained: 'They're going to bring it every gameday. They want to win. It's a winning city and a winning culture.'

SOLDIER FIELD

Nestled on the shores of Lake Michigan, Grant Park Stadium opened in 1924. A year later, its name was changed to Soldier Field in dedication to military personnel who lost their lives in World War I. The 62,500-seat venue, which features notable Doric columns, first served as the home of the Chicago Cardinals before the Bears moved in for the 1971 season, since then more than $630 million of renovations have brought a new look to a historic site.

BEN JOHNSON

The Bears are led by one of the most exciting young coaches in the NFL in Ben Johnson, who was hired away from the Detroit Lions in January 2025. The 39-year-old Johnson got his NFL coaching break with the Miami Dolphins in 2012 before joining the Lions in 2019. He took charge of Detroit's offense in 2022 and led the league's most prolific attack in 2024 as Detroit averaged 33.2 points per game. During his time with the Lions, Johnson earned a reputation for being an innovative and aggressive play-caller who was not afraid to take chances under the leadership of Dan Campbell. The former high-school and college quarterback now gets to forge his own path as a first-time head coach.

JAYLON JOHNSON – CORNERBACK

The Bears have added a wealth of offensive talent in recent times, but the best player on their roster might just reside on the other side of the ball in all-star cornerback Jaylon Johnson. The 2020 second-round draft pick shadowed some of the league's best receivers in a breakout 2023 campaign, grabbing a career-high four interceptions to earn a contract extension worth $76 million in 2024, a year in which he once again earned all-star honours. Johnson's greatest strengths are being able to use his intelligence to read where the quarterback is throwing and then reacting when the ball is in the air, making life tough for opposing receivers. The latest defensive star to don a Bears uniform is well aware of the standard expected of him, as Johnson revealed: 'I knew a lot of the dogs they had. I definitely know the history and tradition of the Bears. That sets a high bar for when you come here.'

WALTER PAYTON – RUNNING BACK

Walter Payton's impact on the Bears and the rest of the NFL was perfectly summed up five days before Christmas in 1987, ahead of the final regular season game of his Hall of Fame career. A banner hanging at Soldier Field for the contest against the Seattle Seahawks read, 'Santa, please send more Walter Paytons. First one was perfect.' Payton – who was nicknamed 'Sweetness' for his demeanour off the field – was Chicago's sensational running back for 13 seasons, being named to the NFL's All-Decade Teams of the 1970s and 1980s. Payton was a smooth, elusive and electric runner who was rarely contained. He was also an excellent receiver in the passing game but what was often overlooked was his physicality, which was hugely respected within the sport. Los Angeles Rams Hall of Fame defensive end Jack Youngblood said: 'Pound for pound, Walter Payton was the toughest who played in our era.' Payton retired with an NFL-record 16,726 rushing yards and set the single-game rushing mark with 275 yards against the Minnesota Vikings in 1977. The Super Bowl champion tragically died of cancer in 1999 at the age of 45.

THE 1985 BEARS

Despite failing to match the achievements of the 1972 Miami Dolphins, by recording the second perfect season in NFL history, the 1985 Chicago Bears – who suffered just one defeat to the Dolphins – are often touted as the greatest ever. The Bears were loaded with talent, particularly on defense, where that unit is also proclaimed to be the best in history. The 1985 Bears were about more than talent, though. They boasted a squad filled with larger-than-life characters who became global stars. Controversial quarterback Jim McMahon, star running back Walter 'Sweetness' Payton and gap-toothed rookie defensive tackle William 'The Refrigerator' Perry were not only driving forces of Chicago's success in America, they were key figures in the growth of the NFL in the UK in the 1980s. Super Bowl 20 against the New England Patriots was powered by one of NFL history's most bullying defensive displays as the Bears won 46-10. Recalling his historic Bears, head coach Mike Ditka said: 'We were one of the greatest teams in NFL history. They were a group of characters who had character. They had backbone, they stood for something. Our players didn't take any prisoners – they played hard. I loved the way they played.'

★ DID YOU KNOW? ★

During the 1985 season, the Bears released an iconic music video called the 'Super Bowl Shuffle'. While there was no problem with the team's star players showing off their rapping and dancing skills, the timing of the recording could have been better. It was made the morning after their only loss of the season against Miami in December. Fortunately, the Bears never lost again. Former defensive back Leslie Frazier said: 'We were a pretty cocky group of guys, but we were able to back it up.'

DALLAS COWBOYS

FIRST SEASON
1960

DIVISION
NFC East

COLOURS
**Navy blue,
metallic silver,
royal blue,
silver-green
and white**

OWNER
Jerry Jones

HEAD COACH
**Brian
Schottenheimer**

STADIUM
**AT&T Stadium
(80,000)**

NFL TITLES/SUPER BOWLS:
**5 (1971, 1977,
1992, 1993, 1995)**

INTRODUCING THE COWBOYS . . .

The Dallas Cowboys are the NFL's most high-profile franchise, with legions of fans spread across the United States, earning them the nickname 'America's Team'. Since their formation in 1960, the Cowboys have grown to become a global brand and the most expensive sports team on the planet, with an estimated value of more than $11 billion.

The Cowboys have enjoyed great success, playing in eight Super Bowls (second-most in NFL history) and lifting the Vince Lombardi Trophy on five occasions (second-most for any team). They were at the height of their powers in the 1990s, winning Super Bowls in the 1992, 1993 and 1995 campaigns behind a high-powered attack led by the Hall of Fame trio of quarterback Troy Aikman, running back Emmitt Smith and wide receiver Michael Irvin. But a barren spell has followed. There have been no titles added since that 1995 season, despite making regular trips to the playoffs.

Today's offense is most dangerous when Dallas are throwing the ball. Quarterback Dak Prescott is a three-time all-star who is among the highest-paid players in league history at $60 million per season, while his favourite target, CeeDee Lamb, has become one of the most electrifying receivers in the league, recording more than 100 catches in each of the 2022, 2023 and 2024 seasons.

The Cowboys are a star-studded outfit filled with all the glitz and glamour you would associate with the NFL and the larger-than-life state of Texas. But the clock is ticking for this talented team and there is pressure to add another Super Bowl to the trophy cabinet.

HOME

AT&T STADIUM

AT&T Stadium opened in 2009 and the 80,000-seat venue, known as 'Jerry World' in a nod to owner Jerry Jones, can expand capacity to more than 100,000 for special events. This was the case for Super Bowl 45, as 103,219 fans saw the Green Bay Packers defeat the Pittsburgh Steelers to conclude the 2010 campaign. The stadium will host a tournament-high nine matches at the 2026 FIFA World Cup, including one of the semi-finals.

HEAD COACH

BRIAN SCHOTTENHEIMER

Brian Schottenheimer became an NFL head coach for the first time when he took charge of the Cowboys in January 2025. The 51-year-old, who is the son of former NFL head coach Marty Schottenheimer (21 seasons leading the Cleveland Browns, Washington, San Diego Chargers and Kansas City Chiefs), spent the 2023 and 2024 seasons overseeing the Dallas attack as the team's offensive coordinator. After promoting the former high-school and college quarterback, Cowboys owner Jerry Jones said: 'I looked at 25 years of being on many staffs in the NFL. I looked at sitting around that dinner table with his daddy, Marty Schottenheimer, and I know what osmosis does. It doesn't fall far from the tree.'

MICAH PARSONS – OUTSIDE LINEBACKER

Being the quarterback of America's Team means Dak Prescott is in the spotlight every weekend, but cast your eyes away from the Cowboys' attack and in the direction of their defense and you will find one of the NFL's most elite players in Micah Parsons. While his primary job is to attack quarterbacks from the edge of the defensive line, Parsons has the versatility to be used all over the formation. A human chess piece in the tactical world of American football, if you will. Parsons flies around the field with explosive menace and is at his very best harassing the superstar passers of the NFL. In his first four seasons in the league, Parsons has proven himself to be a dominant defender, recording 52½ quarterback sacks in his first 63 games. He is universally lauded as one of the best players in the game and is virtually unblockable when on top form, which is pretty much every Sunday. Having burst onto the NFL scene in such destructive fashion, Parsons is already being discussed as an all-time great, drawing comparisons with legendary New York Giants pass rusher Lawrence Taylor, who is widely regarded as one of the greatest defenders in American football history.

EMMITT SMITH – RUNNING BACK

When the Cowboys won three Super Bowls in the early 1990s, their heartbeat was Hall of Fame running back Emmitt Smith, who remains the most prolific runner of all time. From 1991–2001, Smith unleashed 11 straight 1,000-yard seasons and led the NFL in rushing yards in four of five years from 1991 to 1995. Smith was a durable and powerful workhorse back and one who was tough to tackle and impossible to take out of a game plan. Former New England Patriots head coach Bill Belichick once told Smith: 'I've never seen anybody take so many two-yard gains and turn them into eight-yard plays.' After spending 13 of his 15 seasons with the Cowboys, Smith retired having rushed for 18,355 yards and 164 touchdowns. Those are both record marks that still stand today. In addition to Hall of Fame honours, Smith was named to the NFL's 100th Anniversary Team in 2019.

THE FIRST HAIL MARY!

As five-time NFL champions, the Cowboys have enjoyed plenty of highlights. But one special play – which came in a season when Dallas did not lift the Vince Lombardi Trophy – stands out as one of the most talked-about in NFL history. A moment that led to a term we regularly hear in the modern-day game . . . the Hail Mary. The Cowboys took on the defending NFC champion Minnesota Vikings away from home in the first round of the 1975 season playoffs. Dallas trailed 14-10 and had the ball at midfield with 32 seconds remaining. Head coach Tom Landry said: 'Our only hope was to throw and hope for a miracle.' Quarterback Roger Staubach threw the ball as high as he could down the right sideline and wide receiver Drew Pearson caught the ball at the five-yard line and jogged into the end zone to steal a miraculous victory. Staubach later recalled his post-game locker room exchanges with the media: 'They asked me, "What were you thinking about when you threw the ball?" I said, "When I closed my eyes I said a Hail Mary." ' And so, the term for throwing a high desperation pass – often at the end of a half or a game – was born.

★ **DID YOU KNOW?** ★

The Cowboys hold the NFL record for the most consecutive winning seasons in league history with 20 from 1966 to 1985. During that period, they made the playoffs 18 times and reached five Super Bowls.

CHAPTER 09

DETROIT LIONS

FIRST SEASON
1930

DIVISION
NFC North

COLOURS
**Honolulu blue,
silver, white
and black**

OWNER
**Sheila Ford
Hamp**

HEAD COACH
Dan Campbell

STADIUM
**Ford Field
(65,000)**

NFL TITLES/SUPER BOWLS:
**4 (1935, 1952,
1953, 1957)**

INTRODUCING THE LIONS . . .

The Detroit Lions have undergone a remarkable transformation, growing from one of the league's biggest and longest-reigning strugglers to true Super Bowl contenders.

Formed as the Portsmouth Spartans in Ohio in 1930, the franchise fell on hard times and was moved to Detroit in 1934. With the Tigers already established as the city's Major League Baseball squad, the Lions were born. And success quickly followed with a first NFL championship in 1935.

With superstar quarterback Bobby Layne at the helm, Detroit won three more titles in the 1950s. But shockingly, Layne was traded to the Pittsburgh Steelers in 1958 and he remarked that the Lions would 'not win for 50 years'. It became known as The Curse of Bobby Layne.

Layne was onto something. Detroit's next playoff win came at the end of the 1991 season. And the one after that did not come until the end of 2023 – a campaign that saw the reborn Lions reach the NFC Championship Game. A low point in between saw Detroit lose all 16 of their games in 2008. The Lions are the only team that has existed for the entirety of the Super Bowl era not to have appeared in the big game.

But there is great hope under inspirational head coach Dan Campbell, who has coaxed quarterback Jared Goff into the form of his life. And there are talented players everywhere you look, from wide receiver Amon-Ra St.Brown to defensive end Aidan Hutchinson. The modern-day Lions, who won 15 of 17 regular season games in 2024, have roared the ghosts of their past into submission and are threatening to become kings of the NFL.

FORD FIELD

The 65,000-seat Ford Field opened in 2002 in downtown Detroit. The stadium's design incorporates a former warehouse that was built in the 1920s by Hudson's department store. The majority of the stadium's luxury suites are actually situated within the old warehouse. In order to avoid dominance of the Detroit skyline, the playing field is sunk 45 feet below street level. Natural light enters the dome through huge skylights and large glass windows in open corners.

DAN CAMPBELL

Dan Campbell was a tough and uncompromising tight end who played 11 seasons with the New York Giants, Dallas Cowboys, Detroit Lions and New Orleans Saints from 1999 to 2009. He is no different as head coach of the Lions – a position he has held since 2021. In fact, Campbell may have dialed it up a notch or two on the sidelines. He regularly delivers fiery and emotional speeches and few head coaches gamble as much by running plays on fourth down instead of kicking the ball away to the opposition. All of that means that Campbell's players would run through walls for him, and he said of his leadership approach: 'Be true to yourself and be true to the way you were raised. Forget what anybody else thinks of you and treat everybody equally. It doesn't matter if it's somebody who's cleaning the building, picking up trash or it's the owner of the Detroit Lions. You treat them all the same. That's what culture is. It's how you treat people.'

JAHMYR GIBBS – RUNNING BACK

When it comes to deciding who is Detroit's biggest star, there are plenty of candidates – particularly on an offense that was the NFL's most prolific during the 2024 season. And there is a strong case to be made for 23-year-old running back Jahmyr Gibbs, who is an explosive threat to score a touchdown every time he touches the football. In each of his first two NFL seasons – in 2023 and 2024 – Gibbs averaged more than five yards per carry. A good standard for a running back across the NFL would be four yards per attempt. In 2024, Gibbs established himself as one of the league's brightest young stars, scoring 22 touchdowns for the Lions. The first-round draft pick from 2023 looks set to shine in Detroit for years to come. And it doesn't matter that Gibbs is one of the league's quieter players – his action on the field does more than enough talking!

BARRY SANDERS – RUNNING BACK

Barry Sanders was not a physically imposing running back at 5-foot-8 and 200 pounds, but few players across the league struck as much fear into the opposition as Detroit's diminutive Hall of Famer. Long-time NFL linebacker Takeo Spikes once said: 'The one thing I always hoped when we played Detroit was that I wouldn't end up on a Barry Sanders highlight reel.' That was a hard thing to avoid, given that Sanders' entire career was filled with one big play after another. It was often said that Sanders would be impossible to tackle in a phone box. His low centre of gravity meant he could cut on a dime and change direction in a split second. His famous spin moves would leave the greatest defenders in the game trailing in his wake. Sanders played for the Lions from 1989 until his shock retirement in 1998 at the age of 31. At the time, the 10-time all-star stood just 1,457 yards shy of Walter Payton's all-time rushing yards record. His best season came in 1997, when he became just the third player in NFL history to rush for more than 2,000 yards, registering 2,053 on his way to being named the league's Most Valuable Player.

THE LONG WAIT ENDS

As the Lions faced the Los Angeles Rams in the first round of the 2023 season's NFC playoffs, there was an electric atmosphere in Detroit. The Lions were looking to secure their first playoff win since the 1991 campaign and former legends such as running back Barry Sanders and wide receiver Calvin 'Megatron' Johnson were on hand to lend their support, along with Detroit native Eminem. Defensive end Aidan Hutchinson said: 'I had two things I was playing for: I was playing for my teammates and I was playing for the city.' Jared Goff threw for 277 yards and one touchdown as Detroit scrapped their way to a long-awaited 24-23 win. In a twist of fate, Goff – who used to play for the Rams – overcame opposing quarterback Matthew Stafford, who spent his first 12 seasons with the Lions. 'That was the best atmosphere I've ever played in,' Goff insisted. 'It means a whole lot to this city. And it's just the beginning for us.' The wait for another playoff victory was not quite so long. One week later, the Lions defeated the Tampa Bay Buccaneers before eventually losing to the San Francisco 49ers in the NFC Championship Game.

★ DID YOU KNOW? ★

Detroit's rushing attack is powered by two extremely productive but very different running backs in the speedy and electrifying Jahmyr Gibbs and the pounding and powerful David Montgomery. Together they are known as 'Sonic and Knuckles' from the Sonic the Hedgehog video game series. Gibbs, of course, plays the 'Sonic' role and Montgomery's bruising approach makes him the perfect 'Knuckles'. In 2024, the pair combined to score 34 touchdowns.

GREEN BAY PACKERS

FIRST SEASON
1919

DIVISION
NFC North

COLOURS
Dark green, gold and white

OWNER
The fans

HEAD COACH
Matt LaFleur

STADIUM
Lambeau Field (81,441)

NFL TITLES/SUPER BOWLS:
13 (1929, 1930, 1931, 1936, 1939, 1944, 1961, 1962, 1965, 1966, 1967, 1996, 2010)

INTRODUCING THE PACKERS ...

The Green Bay Packers are one of the oldest, most iconic and unique teams in American football history, with their existence pre-dating the birth of the NFL in 1920. Formed in 1919, the Packers spent their first two seasons playing against semi-professional clubs across America's Midwest before joining the NFL in 1921.

The Packers have won a record 13 championships – nine before the Super Bowl era and then four Vince Lombardi Trophies. Green Bay won the first two Super Bowls in the 1966 and 1967 seasons before adding titles in the 1996 and 2010 campaigns.

The Packers are steeped in history. The Super Bowl trophy is named after legendary coach Vince Lombardi, who guided Green Bay to five championships in the 1960s. And they have been led by elite quarterbacks such as Bart Starr, Brett Favre and Aaron Rodgers.

The Packers are the only franchise in America's four major sports – American football, baseball, basketball and ice hockey – to be community owned. The fans own and love their team. The waiting list for season tickets features close to 150,000 names, with many waiting decades to get their hands on the prized possessions that are often left in wills and passed from generation to generation.

The team that Packers fans cheer today has taken on key attributes of the past. Green Bay are a genuine contender that has reached the NFC playoffs in five of the previous six seasons and they boast yet another exciting quarterback talent in 26-year-old Jordan Love, who has earned his $55-million-per-year deal by delivering playoff berths in each of his first two seasons as a full-time starter in 2023 and 2024.

HOME

LAMBEAU FIELD

Lambeau Field – named after Packers founder, player and long-time head coach Earl 'Curly' Lambeau – opened in 1957 and is arguably the NFL's most iconic stadium. Green Bay's Super Bowl-winning wide receiver Greg Jennings said: 'There's nothing like Lambeau Field. You feel the presence of the guys who played before you. Walking out of the tunnel in that stadium is a special and emotional experience.' With a seating capacity of 81,441, Lambeau Field is the second-largest NFL stadium in America and one that every fan should visit at least once.

HEAD COACH

MATT LaFLEUR

The Packers are led by former college football receiver and quarterback Matt LaFleur, who quickly established himself as a winning NFL head coach. In his first four seasons leading the Packers (2019–2022), LaFleur won 47 games – second-most in NFL history. LaFleur got his NFL coaching break as an assistant with the Houston Texans in 2008. After spells with Washington, the Atlanta Falcons, the Los Angeles Rams and the Tennessee Titans, he became the 15th head coach in Green Bay's history. The offensive specialist has coached athletes to three NFL Most Valuable Player awards and two Offensive Player of the Year crowns.

JORDAN LOVE – QUARTERBACK

The Packers clearly saw the huge potential in Jordan Love, selecting the young quarterback from Utah State in the first round of the 2020 NFL Draft even though Green Bay legend and future Hall of Famer Aaron Rodgers was firmly entrenched as the team's starter at that time. Love had to be patient and learn on the job as he watched Rodgers win back-to-back league MVP awards in 2020 and 2021. And he was not installed as Green Bay's full-time starter until 2023, when Rodgers moved to the New York Jets. Love shone in the spotlight as he threw for 4,159 yards and 32 touchdowns – and his outstanding performances drew lofty comparisons to . . . Aaron Rodgers. Like his predecessor, Love is an excellent improvisational player who can attack any area of the field with his talented and adaptable arm. And like Rodgers and Favre before him, Love has great respect for his current team, as he admitted: 'It's very special to be a Green Bay Packer. And what makes it so special is the guys who have played here before me. Having some pretty special and talented quarterbacks playing here is a part of the Green Bay Packers' history and tradition. That is definitely something I keep in the back of my head all the time.'

AARON RODGERS – QUARTERBACK

In a precursor to the drama that would unfold in Green Bay in 2020, Aaron Rodgers was picked in the first round of the 2005 NFL Draft, even though future Hall of Famer Brett Favre was the Packers' clear number-one quarterback at that time. Rodgers waited for three seasons before assuming full control. And he quickly became one of the NFL's biggest stars, leading Green Bay to championship glory with a 31-25 win over the Pittsburgh Steelers in Super Bowl 45 at the end of the 2010 season. Rodgers was named the Most Valuable Player of that game. Ice-cool and blessed with incredible athleticism, arm strength and accuracy, Rodgers is the complete package and one of the greatest quarterbacks the NFL has ever seen. He won four league MVP crowns during 18 glorious seasons in Green Bay before moving to the New York Jets in 2023. Rodgers relished his time with the Packers, as he explained in 2022: 'No player has been in Green Bay longer than I have, as far as years played. And we've had some iconic names from Bart Starr to Brett Favre, Reggie White to Ray Nitschke, Curly Lambeau and Vince Lombardi. To be mentioned forever in connection with this team, that's special.'

THE ICE BOWL

The NFL Championship Game played on New Year's Eve in 1967 would decide whether the Green Bay Packers or the Dallas Cowboys advanced to the second Super Bowl. But it also went down as one of the most famous games in NFL history . . . and the coldest! The temperature at kick-off was -13 degrees Fahrenheit with a wind chill of -48 degrees. When the covers came off at Lambeau Field, the turf instantly froze as hard as rock. Cowboys running back Walt Garrison recalled: 'It was like playing on a frozen pond.' Green Bay made a fast start to lead 14-0 on two touchdown passes from quarterback Bart Starr. Dallas fought back and it was 14-10 at the break when TV commentator Frank Gifford remarked: 'I'm going to have a bite of my coffee now.' Dallas held a 17-14 lead until the final minutes of the game. Starr moved his team downfield with a series of short throws before diving into the end zone with 13 seconds left for a 21-17 victory. The frozen Packers fans – which included a 12-year-old Willem Dafoe attending his first game – stormed the field in celebration and tore down the goalposts. Green Bay became the first team to win three NFL championships in a row and completed their season with a 33-14 thrashing of the Oakland Raiders in Super Bowl 2.

★ DID YOU KNOW? ★

Many Packers players jump into the stands to celebrate with their fans after scoring a touchdown. The tradition known as the Lambeau Leap was spontaneously created by safety LeRoy Butler in 1993 after he scored a Boxing Day touchdown against the Los Angeles Raiders. In 2000, the NFL banned excessive touchdown celebrations but made an exception for the Packers and their unique tradition.

LOS ANGELES RAMS

FIRST SEASON
1936

DIVISION
NFC West

COLOURS
Blue, gold, dark gold, yellow and white

OWNER
E. Stanley Kroenke

HEAD COACH
Sean McVay

STADIUM
SoFi Stadium (70,240)

NFL TITLES/SUPER BOWLS:
4 (1945, 1951, 1999, 2021)

LOS ANGELES RAMS

INTRODUCING THE RAMS . . .

The Los Angeles Rams are one of the NFL's oldest and more well-travelled teams, and they have enjoyed success wherever they have played, winning two NFL championships and two Super Bowls across three cities.

The franchise formed as the Cleveland Rams began playing in the rival American Football League in 1936 before joining the NFL in 1937. The Rams won their first championship in Cleveland in 1945. The Rams played in Los Angeles from 1946 to 1994, winning a second title in 1951. They called St. Louis home from 1995 to 2015, grabbing a Super Bowl crown in the 1999 season before returning to California in 2016, winning a second Vince Lombardi Trophy at the end of the 2021 campaign.

Under the leadership of inspirational coach Sean McVay, the Rams have been one of the NFL's leading teams since returning to Los Angeles. Over the past eight seasons, the Rams have enjoyed seven winning campaigns, reached the playoffs six times, and played in two Super Bowls, losing Super Bowl 53 to the New England Patriots before beating the Cincinnati Bengals in Super Bowl 56.

Following the retirement of Aaron Donald, one of the best defenders in NFL history, at the end of the 2023 season, the Rams have remained competitive behind an explosive attack that perfectly blends experience and youth. Quarterback Matthew Stafford (37) and wide receiver Davante Adams (32) are very well supported by another wideout in Puka Nacua (24) and running back Kyren Williams (25). There is also youthful talent on the other side of the ball, led by 2024 NFL Defensive Rookie of the Year linebacker Jared Verse.

HOME

SoFi STADIUM

Opened in 2020, SoFi Stadium is considered the gold standard of NFL venues. The stadium seats more than 70,000 fans, but can expand to 100,000, as was the case when the Rams won Super Bowl 56 in front of their own supporters during the 2021 season. While it may look like a dome at first glance, SoFi Stadium is an open-air venue covered by a translucent canopy. The site will host Super Bowl 61 in the 2026 season.

HEAD COACH

SEAN McVAY

Hired in 2017 as the youngest head coach in the NFL's modern era at 30, Sean McVay has been hugely successful in L.A., delivering seven winning seasons out of eight, earning NFL Coach of the Year honours and securing Super Bowl glory. He has paved the way for more young coaches to lead teams of their own, with it often being reported that NFL franchises are 'looking for the next Sean McVay'. The former high-school quarterback is an incredible offensive play designer and play-caller, but McVay's energy might be his greatest attribute. He routinely begins his workdays around 3am and said: 'Any time you're able to do something that you love, you wake up every morning and you feel excited about the opportunity. This is a chance to help people reach their highest potential. That's what makes great coaches.'

PUKA NACUA – WIDE RECEIVER

While he enjoyed a solid college career at Washington and then Brigham Young University, there weren't huge expectations placed upon Puka Nacua's young shoulders. After all, the 24-year-old entered the NFL as an overlooked fifth-round pick in 2023 and the Rams already had a reliable veteran leading the way at wide receiver in Super Bowl 56 Most Valuable Player Cooper Kupp. But Nacua became an instant star in Los Angeles, setting NFL rookie records with 105 catches for 1,486 yards. He backed that up with another 990 receiving yards in 2024, despite missing six games through injury. The receiver, who is of Samoan and Hawaiian descent, is the complete package – he can make tough receptions over the middle of the field, reel in spectacular catches and also sprint away from defenders, even though 'Puka' is Samoan for fat and chubby.

AARON DONALD – DEFENSIVE TACKLE

In the middle of a career that saw him shine bright from 2014 to 2023, Los Angeles Rams defensive tackle Aaron Donald said: 'I don't play this game to be average. I play this game to be great and to be one of the best to ever do it.' It was mission accomplished for the three-time NFL Defensive Player of the Year, who was often unplayable. Donald was never the biggest of defensive linemen at 6-foot-1 and 280 pounds, but he was cat-quick, violent and a bowling ball of domination even though he was constantly double-teamed by opposing offensive linemen. Often hailed by his peers to be the best player in the NFL regardless of position, Donald recorded 111 sacks in 10 seasons. The biggest play of his career was not a sack, but a pressure of Cincinnati Bengals quarterback Joe Burrow in Super Bowl 56. Cincinnati trailed 23-20 and faced a fourth down at the Rams' 49-yard line with 43 seconds remaining. The season was on the line for both teams. On the sideline, Rams head coach Sean McVay said: 'For the world championship right here . . . Aaron Donald's gonna make a play.' It was a solid prediction. Within seconds, Donald sped around the end of the line and spun Burrow to the ground. All the Bengals' quarterback could do was fling the ball incomplete, crowning the Rams as NFL champions. Donald retired at the end of 2023 having been an NFL all-star in all 10 of his seasons.

THE TACKLE

In the 1999 season, the Rams won their first Super Bowl with a 23-16 win over the Tennessee Titans. In a reminder of sport's fine margins, Super Bowl 34 was decided by one yard and by the most famous tackle in NFL history. The Rams boasted the NFL's best attack, known as 'The Greatest Show on Turf', featuring NFL MVP Kurt Warner at quarterback, Marshall Faulk at running back and dynamic receivers in Isaac Bruce and Torry Holt. But it was an unheralded defender who secured glory. With six seconds left, Tennessee had time for one play from the Rams' 10-yard line, needing a touchdown to force overtime. Steve McNair completed a short pass to Kevin Dyson at the four-yard line and the receiver was immediately wrapped up by linebacker Mike Jones, who hung on for dear life. Dyson stretched every muscle to reach the end zone but came up short. Game over! It was the defining moment of Jones' 13-year career. When reflecting on his moment in the spotlight, Jones laughed and told *Bleacher Report*: 'Everyone asks, "Does it bother you that you're known for making one play?" It could be a whole lot worse. I could be known for missing the tackle.'

★ DID YOU KNOW? ★

While Rams fans enjoy watching Super Bowl-winning all-star quarterback Matthew Stafford shine on Sundays, they also play 'Spot the Celebrity' at SoFi Stadium. Being based in Los Angeles, the NFC West club boasts a star-studded fan base that includes basketball star LeBron James, actors Ty Burrell (*Modern Family*) and Bryan Cranston (*Breaking Bad*), and rapper and record producer Snoop Dogg.

MINNESOTA VIKINGS

FIRST SEASON
1961

DIVISION
NFC North

COLOURS
Purple, gold and white

OWNER
Zygi, Mark and Leonard Wilf

HEAD COACH
Kevin O'Connell

STADIUM
U.S. Bank Stadium (66,860)

NFL TITLES/SUPER BOWLS:
0

INTRODUCING THE VIKINGS . . .

The Minnesota Vikings are one of the most successful teams never to win a Super Bowl or to be crowned NFL champions. In their first 64 years, the competitive Vikings won 21 division titles and made 32 trips to the playoffs, powered by some of the greatest players in league history.

But ultimate glory has eluded these NFL nearly-men. Minnesota lost four Super Bowls in eight seasons from 1969 to 1976 – a period that featured Hall of Famer Fran Tarkenton at quarterback and a feared defense that was known as 'The Purple People Eaters'. On seven other occasions, the Vikings have fallen one game short of the Super Bowl. Their most recent disappointment in the NFC Championship Game came at the end of the 2017 season, with defeat to the Philadelphia Eagles.

The Vikings were driven to the 2024 playoffs by resurgent veteran quarterback Sam Darnold, who turned a career-defining year into a fresh start with the Seattle Seahawks. And that means the Vikings are now led by 2024 first-round quarterback J.J. McCarthy, who missed his entire rookie campaign with a knee injury. The young passer who won a college football national championship at the University of Michigan has exciting weapons around him, led by the dynamic wide receiver pairing of Justin Jefferson and Jordan Addison, all-star tight end T.J. Hockenson and veteran running back Aaron Jones.

U.S. BANK STADIUM

The Vikings play at the stunning U.S. Bank Stadium. The 66,860-seat venue opened in 2016 and hosted Super Bowl 52 between the Philadelphia Eagles and New England Patriots at the end of the 2017 season. The fixed-roof stadium designed to keep out Minnesota's freezing conditions has also hosted the ESPN X Games, the NCAA basketball Final Four and soccer friendlies featuring Tottenham Hotspur, Chelsea and AC Milan.

KEVIN O'CONNELL

Kevin O'Connell is a former backup quarterback who threw just six career passes with the New England Patriots and New York Jets. As a New England player, O'Connell learned from the great Bill Belichick and admitted: 'I do think back on the coaching seed being planted there, just having seen what I call Football 501 – the highest level of coaching you can be around.' O'Connell won a Super Bowl as an assistant with the Los Angeles Rams before taking charge of the Vikings in 2022. The 40-year-old has been praised for being a renowned offensive tactician who has created a tremendous locker room culture.

JUSTIN JEFFERSON – WIDE RECEIVER

Justin Jefferson was ranked by one scouting service as the 308th-best wide receiver in America when he was in high school and saw five players at his position taken ahead of him in the opening round of the 2020 NFL Draft. But Jefferson is no longer overlooked and is universally regarded as the best receiver in the NFL today. The 26-year-old, who regularly makes science-defying, breathtaking catches, is not about to rest on his laurels and often recalls how he was not as highly rated in his recent past. 'I definitely keep that in mind,' the Louisiana native admitted. 'You've always got to keep that chip on your shoulder. I was the 308th receiver then and now I'm number one – that's crazy.' Jefferson was voted a Pro Bowl all-star in four of his first five years in the NFL and amassed the most receiving yards in a player's first five seasons in league history (7,432), topping legends such as Randy Moss and Jerry Rice. Jefferson is one of the biggest stars in the NFL and his 'Griddy' touchdown dance has become iconic and beloved, much to his own surprise, as Minnesota's star man laughed: 'It's unbelievable how far the "Griddy" has come. The whole world is doing the "Griddy"!'

FRAN TARKENTON – QUARTERBACK

In an era when running the ball was still the dominant way of moving downfield, Fran Tarkenton was the NFL's most prolific passer. And, ironically, the nine-time all-star, who was named the league's Most Valuable Player in 1975, exposed defenses with his ability to move away from pressure, circling from one side of the field to the other before throwing accurate passes to his receivers. Tarkenton, who was nicknamed 'The Scrambler', played for the Vikings from their inaugural 1961 season until he was traded to the New York Giants in 1967. The dual-threat legend, who scored at least one rushing touchdown in 15 of his 18 NFL seasons, was traded back to Minnesota in 1972 and guided the team to three of its four Super Bowl visits. At the time of his retirement in 1978, Tarkenton held every major passing record in the book, including yards (47,003) and touchdowns (342).

THE MINNEAPOLIS MIRACLE

The 2017 Minnesota Vikings entered the playoffs dreaming of hosting Super Bowl 52 in their own stadium. But in their NFC Divisional Round contest with the New Orleans Saints, hopes were fading. Minnesota blew a 17-0 lead and trailed 24-23 after the Saints kicked a field goal with 25 seconds remaining. The Vikings – led by journeyman quarterback Case Keenum – had one last shot to save their season. With 10 seconds left, Minnesota had time for one play from their own 39-yard line. Keenum heaved a high and hopeful pass down the right sideline. It was caught by wide receiver Stefon Diggs. Saints safety Marcus Williams flew straight past Diggs and took out the only other defender in the area. Diggs was free to run down the sideline for the winning touchdown as time expired. Vikings radio announcer Paul Allen screamed: 'Are you kidding me? It's a Minneapolis Miracle!' After Minnesota's stunning 29-24 victory, receiver Adam Thielen said: 'I will never forget that. To win in that fashion, with all those emotions, was special.'

★ DID YOU KNOW? ★

Ahead of Minnesota's home games, the Gjallarhorn is blown to announce that the 'Vikings are Coming' – a tradition started in 2007 and one that has featured club legends Randy Moss, Adrian Peterson, Jared Allen and John Randle. The Vikings are onto a second horn after the first cracked before the 2015 season's home playoff game against the Seattle Seahawks, which was played outside in sub-zero temperatures.

NEW ORLEANS SAINTS

FIRST SEASON
1967

DIVISION
NFC South

COLOURS
Old gold, black, white

OWNER
Gayle Benson

HEAD COACH
Kellen Moore

STADIUM
Caesars Superdome (73,208)

NFL TITLES/SUPER BOWLS:
1 (2009)

NEW ORLEANS SAINTS

INTRODUCING THE SAINTS . . .

New Orleans Saints supporters had their patience severely tested when the team entered the league in 1967. Things were bleak as the Saints opened life in the NFL with 20 straight seasons in which they never posted a winning record.

Legend has it that a disgruntled fan once left two season tickets under the windscreen wipers of their car, hoping they would be taken, thus ending the misery of attending Saints games each weekend. But when the driver returned, there were four season tickets under the wipers! No wonder Saints fans famously attended games with brown paper bags over their heads to hide their embarrassment.

With a group of quarterback-hunting defenders known as The Dome Patrol leading the way, the Saints finally qualified for the playoffs in 1987. But their fortunes really took a dramatic upswing in 2006 when the franchise hired Sean Payton as head coach and signed quarterback Drew Brees from the San Diego Chargers. The pair instantly ignited a run to the NFC Championship Game.

In the 2009 season, the Saints won their lone Super Bowl with a 31-17 victory over the Indianapolis Colts. That kicked off a run during which New Orleans qualified for the playoffs in eight of 12 seasons.

The modern-day Saints are still cheered on by some of the most passionate fans in the NFL, who take the party from Bourbon Street into the Superdome every Sunday. While the Saints have been competitive, they have failed to make the playoffs in each of the past five seasons.

CAESARS SUPERDOME

Opened as the Louisiana Superdome in 1975, this domed stadium in New Orleans' central business district hosted its eighth Super Bowl at the end of the 2024 NFL season as the Philadelphia Eagles defeated the Kansas City Chiefs. In 2005, the Superdome housed thousands of people seeking shelter from Hurricane Katrina. The building suffered extensive damage from the storm, forcing the Saints to play in San Antonio, Texas, and Baton Rouge, Louisiana.

KELLEN MOORE

The son of a former high-school head coach, Kellen Moore spent six seasons as a backup quarterback in the NFL with the Detroit Lions and Dallas Cowboys. He began his coaching career with the Cowboys in 2018, tutoring the club's quarterbacks. Moore took charge of Dallas's attack as offensive coordinator from 2019 to 2022 and held the same position with the Los Angeles Chargers in 2023. He served as offensive coordinator of the Philadelphia Eagles in 2024 and helped that team score 95 total points in the NFC Championship Game win over Washington and the Super Bowl 59 defeat of Kansas City. Two days after that title-winning victory in New Orleans, the 37-year-old committed his immediate future to the city by becoming head coach of the Saints.

ALVIN KAMARA – RUNNING BACK

Alvin Kamara is the Saints' most dynamic weapon and he is the most productive running back in team history. Chosen by the Saints in the third round of the 2017 NFL Draft, Kamara is still going strong as one of the most versatile backs in the game today. What has made Kamara so good over the years is his ability to do the most important thing for any player – he regularly gets into the end zone with the football. In his first 100 career games, Kamara scored an impressive 77 touchdowns. The five-time all-star was at his prolific best on Christmas Day in 2020 when wearing a red shoe on his right foot and a green one on his left and scoring an NFL record-tying six touchdowns in a 52-33 win over the Minnesota Vikings. Brees said of his teammate's performance: 'It was awesome. Six touchdowns for a running back is just astounding.' Kamara is the ideal modern-day running back who is hard to defend. When he gets to the edges, the 30-year-old is tough to bring down in space. But he is equally adept at gaining the hard yards when attacking the middle of a defense, making him the complete player.

DREW BREES – QUARTERBACK

Drew Brees was a good quarterback when he played for the San Diego Chargers from 2001 to 2005. He became a great one as the leader of the New Orleans Saints from 2006 until his retirement at the end of the 2020 season, when he left the stage as one of the best the NFL has ever seen. Throughout NFL history, there have been just 15 occasions where quarterbacks have thrown for more than 5,000 yards in a season. And Brees accomplished that feat a league-leading five times. Relatively small for a quarterback at 6-foot and 209 pounds, Brees destroyed opposing defenses with his quick-thinking brain and his accurate arm. He was named Most Valuable Player of Super Bowl 44 as the Saints beat the Indianapolis Colts 31-17 at the end of the 2009 season. Brees worked brilliantly with head coach Sean Payton to lead a Saints attack that was one of the best in the league year in and year out. He retired as the owner of some of the NFL's most prestigious records, with 6,017 career completions, 68,010 passing yards and 491 passing touchdowns.

MOMENT IN TIME

THE ONSIDE KICK

The Saints conjured up one of the most famous plays in Super Bowl history against the favoured Indianapolis Colts. Trailing 10-6 at the break of Super Bowl 44, head coach Sean Payton called 'Ambush' – an onside kick designed to steal a possession from the Colts via the boot of punter Thomas Morstead. The plan was for the Saints to open the second half with a short kick that would barely travel the required 10 yards, while Indianapolis would be expecting a traditional kick deep to the goal-line. As soon as the ball passed 10 yards, it was live and either team could recover it. The problem was that the then-rookie Morstead was told about the plan at the end of the first half and had an agonising wait of between 25 and 30 minutes due to the Super Bowl halftime show. The 'terrified' Morstead then delivered the perfect misdirection kick, which was recovered by safety Chris Reis, turning the tide in New Orleans' favour. Moments later, the Saints took their first lead through Pierre Thomas and went on to win 31-17, with the game being sealed by Tracy Porter's interception of the great Peyton Manning, which was returned for a touchdown.

★ **DID YOU KNOW?** ★

Northern Ireland's Charlie Smyth is a kicker for the New Orleans Saints, having joined the team via the NFL's International Player Pathway programme. Smyth, from Newry, County Down, previously played Gaelic football as a goalkeeper. He was a big NFL fan even before signing with the Saints, listing quarterback Aaron Rodgers among his favourite players.

NEW YORK GIANTS

FIRST SEASON
1925

DIVISION
NFC East

COLOURS
Dark blue, red and white

OWNERS
John Mara and Steve Tisch

HEAD COACH
Brian Daboll

STADIUM
MetLife Stadium (82,500)

NFL TITLES/SUPER BOWLS:
8 (1927, 1934, 1938, 1956, 1986, 1990, 2007, 2011)

NEW YORK GIANTS

INTRODUCING THE GIANTS . . .

The New York Giants are one of the oldest and most decorated teams in American football history. Joining the NFL in 1925 – five years after the league's formation – the Giants won four pre-Super Bowl-era titles in 1927, 1934, 1938 and 1956. They added four Super Bowl wins in the 1986, 1990, 2007 and 2011 seasons, taking their NFL championship tally to eight – third-best in league history behind the Green Bay Packers (13) and Chicago Bears (nine).

While their last two Super Bowl successes featured outstanding performances from quarterback Eli Manning, the Giants are a team steeped in a rich defensive tradition. Some of the greatest defenders in NFL history have played for the Big Blue, including linebackers Lawrence Taylor, Harry Carson and Sam Huff – all of whom are members of the Pro Football Hall of Fame.

And there are stars on that side of the ball today in the form of Dexter Lawrence, Brian Burns and Kayvon Thibodeaux, who all specialise in pressuring opposing quarterbacks.

The current Giants feature the explosive Malik Nabers. In his first season in the NFL in 2024, this product of Louisiana State University set a new NFL record for catches by a rookie wide receiver with 109. He represents a brighter future for a team that has a lot of work to do. New York have missed the playoffs with a losing record in seven of their last eight seasons. The lone exception was the 2022 campaign that saw Brian Daboll crowned NFL Coach of the Year as the Giants won 10 games on their way to the second round of the NFC playoffs.

HOME

MetLife STADIUM

The Giants share their home – MetLife Stadium – with the New York Jets. Opened for play in 2010, the 82,500-seat venue is situated in New Jersey, five miles west of downtown Manhattan. While the teams never play at the venue on the same day, they occasionally host home games on the same weekend. It takes approximately 16 hours and more than 250 employees to transform the stadium from Jets to Giants, including new turf artwork, video board content and signage around the venue.

HEAD COACH

BRIAN DABOLL

Brian Daboll is in his fourth season as Giants head coach and is intent on bringing his winning ways to the Big Apple. Daboll entered the NFL coaching ranks as an assistant with the New England Patriots in 2000. He worked three different spells under the great Bill Belichick, winning five Super Bowls. The 49-year-old Daboll has also led the attacks of the Cleveland Browns, Miami Dolphins, Kansas City Chiefs and Buffalo Bills. In 2022, his first season leading his own team, the fiery and emotional Daboll took the Giants to the playoffs, delivered a first-round win at Minnesota and was named NFL Coach of the Year.

DEXTER LAWRENCE – DEFENSIVE TACKLE

Universally described as a one-of-a-kind player, there is no doubt that the 342-pound Dexter Lawrence is the key piece of New York's growing defense. That's why the Giants signed the 26-year-old to a $90 million contract extension in the spring of 2024. Lawrence anchors down in the middle of New York's defensive line and is very hard to contain. The three-time Pro Bowl all-star and two-time All-Pro explodes into action when the ball is snapped and often gets his hands on the center before pushing his opponent back into the quarterback or shedding his blocker to make big plays in the opponent's backfield. Lawrence can mix it up and defend the run like an old-school interior defensive lineman, but his true worth is in chasing quarterbacks. After recording four and a half sacks and 65 quarterback pressures in 2023 and a career-high nine sacks in 2024, Lawrence has truly arrived and his is a name you will hear called time and again when watching the Giants.

LAWRENCE TAYLOR – OUTSIDE LINEBACKER

If you could travel back in time and attend a New York Giants game between 1981 and 1993, you would see thousands of fans sporting number 56 jerseys. You would witness opponents being intimidated from the opening play of the game to the very last and you would be in awe of one of the most destructive defensive forces in NFL history in outside linebacker Lawrence Taylor. The Hall of Famer – who would famously implore his teammates to 'go out and play like a bunch of crazed dogs' – was a force of nature during a career that saw him record 132½ sacks, win two Super Bowls and be named the NFL's Most Valuable Player in 1986 (a reward so often reserved for quarterbacks). L.T. changed the way outside linebacker was played in the NFL. Before Taylor, it was very much a read and react position. The 10-time all-star and three-time NFL Defensive Player of the Year changed it into the aggressive, chase-the-quarterback style we see today through the likes of Pittsburgh's T.J. Watt and Nick Bosa of the San Francisco 49ers. Fellow Hall of Famer and former Minnesota Vikings defensive lineman John Randle said: 'Lawrence Taylor was the Elvis Presley of football.'

THE HELMET CATCH

Sport often throws up unlikely heroes and that was the case for the New York Giants in Super Bowl 42, as little-used wide receiver David Tyree made one of American football's most famous plays. The Giants were heavy underdogs as they took on a New England Patriots team looking to complete just the second perfect season in NFL history. With 75 seconds remaining, the Giants trailed 14-10 and needed a touchdown to win as they faced a key third down from their own 44-yard line. Quarterback Eli Manning was quickly pressured by three defenders. He eluded Adalius Thomas and broke free from the grasp of Jarvis Green and Richard Seymour to throw a hopeful pass downfield. Tyree – who made just four catches during the regular season – leapt to grab the ball while well covered by all-star safety Rodney Harrison. Miraculously, Tyree pinned the ball to his helmet and fell to the ground for a 32-yard gain. Moments later, Manning threw the winning touchdown pass to Plaxico Burress and the surprising Giants were crowned champions of the 2007 season with the 17-14 win. Tyree's moment in the spotlight was fleeting, as The Helmet Catch was his last NFL reception. He said: 'I get back to the hotel and I need to go and see what this thing looks like. I see the catch and my jaw drops. That was the first time in my life I was impressed with my own work.'

★ DID YOU KNOW? ★

Harry Potter is a New York Giants fan! Daniel Radcliffe, who played the lead role in the spectacular movie franchise, got into the NFL by playing Fantasy Football with his friends. After losing his first three games, the ultra-competitive actor decided he needed to learn more and started watching New York Giants games.

PHILADELPHIA EAGLES

FIRST SEASON
1933

OWNER
Jeffrey Lurie

DIVISION
NFC East

HEAD COACH
Nick Sirianni

COLOURS
Midnight green, silver, black and white

STADIUM
Lincoln Financial Field (67,594)

NFL TITLES/SUPER BOWLS:
5 (1948, 1949, 1960, 2017, 2024)

PHILADELPHIA EAGLES

INTRODUCING THE EAGLES . . .

Newcomers looking for an NFL team to follow will be casting a long, hard look in the direction of the Philadelphia Eagles, who were crowned champions of the NFL's 2024 season after defeating the Kansas City Chiefs in Super Bowl 59.

That 40-22 thrashing of the Chiefs showcased everything that is good about a team that should stay in championship contention for years to come. Reigning Super Bowl Most Valuable Player Jalen Hurts is a quarterback capable of dissecting defenses with bold throws, but he is also an outstanding runner who has scored at least 10 rushing touchdowns in each of his four seasons as the full-time starter, guiding Philadelphia to the playoffs on each occasion. Further powering the ground attack is the NFL's best running back in Saquon Barkley, who enjoyed historic success during his first season with the Eagles in 2024. Both work behind the strongest offensive line in the league.

The Eagles also boasted the NFL's top-ranked defense in 2024 and they sacked Chiefs superstar quarterback Patrick Mahomes six times in Super Bowl 59, also intercepting him twice in a dominant display.

Whoever plays for the Eagles, they're going to hear their fans. When they're doing well, players will be cheered to the heavens and celebrated as heroes. But if it goes wrong, their passionate supporters – who once famously booed a charity worker dressed as Santa Claus – are going to express their displeasure.

Supporting the Eagles is a visceral, raw and emotional experience, and the minimum demand for a team based in the city of Rocky Balboa is to play with passion. And the Eagles, who were formed in 1933, have delivered by winning five championships in their history.

HOME

LINCOLN FINANCIAL FIELD

The Eagles opened Lincoln Financial Field to great fanfare in 2003, with Rocky Balboa himself – Sylvester Stallone – on hand to whip the crowd of more than 67,000 fans into a frenzy. The stadium design gives a nod to the team's nickname, with wing-like canopies above the east and west stands and the Eagle's Nest balcony in the north end zone. The venue will host six games at the 2026 FIFA World Cup.

HEAD COACH

NICK SIRIANNI

In many ways, Nick Sirianni is the ideal coach for the Philadelphia Eagles. He is fiery, passionate and wears his heart on his sleeve, as evidenced by the tears streaming down his face during the American national anthem ahead of Super Bowl 57. Sirianni began his NFL coaching career as an assistant with the Kansas City Chiefs in 2010. He also coached with the Los Angeles Chargers before overseeing the Indianapolis Colts' offense from 2018 to 2020. Hired by the Eagles in 2021, Sirianni has taken his team to the playoffs in each of his first four seasons in charge, reached two Super Bowls and delivered a championship in 2024.

SAQUON BARKLEY – RUNNING BACK

Philadelphia's march to glory in Super Bowl 59 actually began in the spring of 2024 – months before the season kicked off – with the free-agent signing of Pro Bowl running back Saquon Barkley. While he was a high-end player with the New York Giants, Barkley exploded to another level with the Eagles. By the end of the 2024 season, Barkley had rushed for a total of 2,504 yards – the most for any player in NFL history; including the playoffs. Along the way, he produced one of the most breath-taking plays in NFL history against the Jacksonville Jaguars as he backward hurdled over the head of 5-foot-11 cornerback Jarrian Jones, who was stood upright at the time. Eagles head coach Nick Sirianni said: 'It was the best play I've ever seen.' Barkley is not only an outstanding player, he's also a great member of Philadelphia's locker room, as tight end Dallas Goedert explained: 'As good as he is as a football player, he's an even better person. It's so cool to see a superstar like that as humble as he is.'

REGGIE WHITE – DEFENSIVE END

Most NFL offensive linemen pride themselves on being strong and hard to move, as they weigh between 320 and 350 pounds and can tower up to 6-foot-7 in height. But those who faced off against the great Reggie White during his Hall of Fame career would often find themselves being thrown around like rag dolls. Known as 'The Minister of Defense' due to him being an ordained minister, White dominated with extreme power. The Tennessee native spent his first eight seasons, from 1985 to 1992, with the Eagles and recorded a stunning 124 sacks in just 121 games. He moved on to win Super Bowl 31 with the Green Bay Packers in the 1996 season, registering a record three sacks against the New England Patriots. White – who retired in 2000 – would often club offensive linemen to the side with one powerful hand on his way to what was an NFL record 198 career sacks at the time of his retirement. Speaking about his approach to the game, White said: 'When I'm on the field, I'm going to do my best to intimidate the guy in front of me.' Tragically, White died of heart issues on 26 December 2004, at the age of 43.

THE PHILLY SPECIAL

In Super Bowl 52, the Eagles produced a play so stunning that they built a statue outside of Lincoln Financial Field to forever commemorate the catalyst for a dramatic 41-33 victory over the New England Patriots. Late in the first half, the Eagles led 15-12 and faced a fourth down at New England's one-yard line. Rather than kick a field goal, Philadelphia called a time out and planned to go for the touchdown. Backup quarterback Nick Foles asked head coach Doug Pederson: 'You want Philly Philly?' Pederson stared into his player's eyes for a second and then replied: 'Yeah, let's do it.' The trick play saw Foles pretend to move off the original play call as he screamed 'kill, kill' while moving towards the right side of the line. The ball was snapped to running back Corey Clement, who flipped it to tight end Trey Burton, who threw a touchdown pass to a wide-open Foles to give the Eagles a 10-point lead at the break. Former NFL receiver-turned TV commentator Cris Collinsworth said: 'That play call has a chance to be remembered as one of the all-time greats.' Reflecting on the pivotal moment, Pederson said: 'You don't just flip a switch and say we're going to run The Philly Special. There is a lot of coaching and preparation for that.' The statue captures the sideline conversation between Foles and his head coach. Speaking of the statue, Pederson joked: 'It's me and Rocky Balboa in the city of Philadelphia.'

★ DID YOU KNOW? ★

One of Philadelphia's best players is Australian tackle Jordan Mailata – a former rugby league player who never played a snap of American football before being drafted by the Eagles in 2018.

SAN FRANCISCO 49ERS

FIRST SEASON
1946

DIVISION
NFC West

COLOURS
Red, gold and white

OWNER
The York Family

HEAD COACH
Kyle Shanahan

STADIUM
Levi's Stadium (68,500)

NFL TITLES/SUPER BOWLS:
5 (1981, 1984, 1988, 1989, 1994)

SAN FRANCISCO 49ERS

INTRODUCING THE 49ERS . . .

The 49ers are one of the most successful teams in the NFL's modern era, winning five Super Bowls (second-most). They were dubbed 'Team of the 80s' for their dominance during that decade, winning four Super Bowls (1981, 1984, 1988, 1989) with the legendary Joe Montana at quarterback.

San Francisco won another Super Bowl in the 1994 season with fellow Hall of Famer Steve Young succeeding Montana. But it's been three decades since that success and the 49ers have come frustratingly close to further glory, losing Super Bowls in the 2012, 2019 and 2023 seasons. They also lost in the NFC Championship Game in the 2021 and 2022 campaigns, prompting star tight end George Kittle to say: 'I walk in this building and there are five Super Bowl trophies lined up there. I walk past them every day. I'm very motivated to win. This team is hungry.'

Kittle is one of several big names on a star-studded attack. Christian McCaffrey is among the best running backs in the NFL and wide receiver Brandon Aiyuk is one of the most dynamic in the game.

Distributing the ball to those weapons is one of the best young players – and stories – in the NFL in 25-year-old quarterback Brock Purdy. In the 2022 NFL Draft, Purdy was the last player chosen (262nd overall), earning him the unfortunate nickname of 'Mr Irrelevant'. He has been anything but in his first three seasons in the league, quickly overcoming lengthy odds to become one of the NFL's most productive passers who now earns $53 million per year after inking a new deal in 2025.

HOME

LEVI'S STADIUM
The 49ers' glory years came while playing at iconic Candlestick Park in San Francisco. But the team moved into a new, state-of-the-art venue with Levi's Stadium in 2014. The 68,500-seat stadium is actually located 43 miles south of downtown San Francisco in Santa Clara. The stadium hosted Super Bowl 50 in the 2015 season and will host Super Bowl 60 in the 2025 campaign. It will also host six matches during the 2026 FIFA World Cup.

HEAD COACH

KYLE SHANAHAN
The 49ers are led by one of the NFL's most creative attacking minds in Kyle Shanahan. Former 49ers offensive lineman Joe Staley insists: 'As a play-caller, I've never been around a guy who understands the X's and O's as much as he does. He plays the ultimate chess game with everybody.' The 45-year-old Shanahan grew up around the game, as his father, Mike, won two Super Bowls as head coach of the Denver Broncos in the 1990s. Kyle has guided San Francisco to the playoffs in four of the past six seasons, but has lost two Super Bowls in that time.

CHRISTIAN McCAFFREY – RUNNING BACK

Christian McCaffrey is not only one of the best running backs in the NFL today, he's one of the most complete players to grace the league in quite some time. McCaffrey can do it all. He can run up the middle where the traffic is thickest and the hits can be the hardest. With excellent vision and an ability to spin out of tackles, the three-time all-star is tough to bring down. And when he sprints to the outside, McCaffrey has the pace to run away from the quickest of defenders and can score from anywhere on the field. In 2023, McCaffrey led the NFL with 1,459 rushing yards and was named the league's Offensive Player of the Year. The former Carolina Panthers star, who joined the 49ers in 2022, is also a real danger when catching passes. The 29-year-old is the only running back in NFL history to register two seasons in which he topped 100 catches. And, in 2019, he became just the third player ever to register more than 1,000 rushing yards and 1,000 receiving yards in the same season. The only accolade McCaffrey needs to add to his collection is the Super Bowl ring that his skills and production richly deserve.

JERRY RICE – WIDE RECEIVER

When the 49ers were a powerhouse in the late 1980s and early 1990s, the silky-smooth and impossible-to-cover Jerry Rice was tormenting defenses as the favourite target of Hall of Fame quarterbacks Joe Montana and Steve Young. Rice, who honed his skills catching bricks while working a construction job as a youth, won three Super Bowl rings with San Francisco and earned the original version of the nickname 'GOAT (Greatest Of All Time)' during his 20-year career. After 16 seasons with San Francisco and four with the Oakland Raiders and the Seattle Seahawks, Rice retired with records that may never be broken with 1,549 catches for 22,985 yards. The Hall of Famer, who was renowned for being an incredibly hard worker – often seen running the hills of San Francisco to stay in top shape – also scored the most touchdowns in NFL history with 207. Rice is widely considered the best non-quarterback to play the game.

THE CATCH

Every period of historic dominance has a start and an end. For the 49ers, their spell of ruling the NFL kicked off with one of the sport's most famous plays as Joe Montana and wide receiver Dwight Clark connected on 'The Catch'. The 49ers had never reached a Super Bowl when they hosted the Dallas Cowboys in the 1981 NFC Championship Game. San Francisco trailed 27-21 inside the final minute when Montana ran to his right from the Cowboys' six-yard line and – with three Dallas defenders bearing down on him – threw the ball as high as he could into the end zone. A leaping Clark, who had been running in the opposite direction just seconds earlier, changed direction, mirrored Montana's run and stretched to reel in the iconic catch. The home crowd went wild. Among them, a young Tom Brady, who grew up a 49ers fan and would later go on to win a record seven Super Bowls as a quarterback with New England and Tampa Bay. San Francisco held on for the final 51 seconds to win 28-27 and advanced to Super Bowl 16, where they defeated the Cincinnati Bengals to lift the Vince Lombardi Trophy for the first time.

★ DID YOU KNOW? ★

San Francisco running back Christian McCaffrey is the son of former New York Giants, Denver Broncos and 49ers wide receiver Ed McCaffrey. When Ed played for the 49ers in 1994, Mike Shanahan was the team's offensive coordinator. And Kyle Shanahan – now San Francisco's head coach – would be tasked with babysitting Christian McCaffrey.

SEATTLE SEAHAWKS

FIRST SEASON
1976

DIVISION
NFC West

COLOURS
College navy, action green, wolf grey

OWNER
Paul G. Allen Estate

HEAD COACH
Mike Macdonald

STADIUM
Lumen Field (68,740)

NFL TITLES/SUPER BOWLS:
1 (2013)

INTRODUCING THE SEAHAWKS . . .

The Seahawks have the rare distinction of having played in both the American Football Conference (AFC) and the National Football Conference (NFC) since entering the NFL as an expansion team in 1976. Whether they were in the AFC West (1976–2001) or the NFC West (2002 to modern day), this team has and always will be cheered on by some of the loudest fans in world sport.

Home games at Seattle are a visceral, noisy experience and you'd be advised to bring your earplugs! In 2013, Seahawks fans broke the *Guinness Book of World Records* mark for the loudest crowd at a sports event as they roared to 137.6 decibels in a game against the New Orleans Saints.

The Seahawks have given their fans plenty to cheer about, reaching three Super Bowls in the 2005, 2013 and 2014 seasons. Under the guidance of legendary head coach Pete Carroll, Seattle qualified for the playoffs 10 times from 2010 to 2022 and won Super Bowl 48 with a 43-8 demolition of the Denver Broncos at the end of that 2013 campaign.

The Seahawks have embarked on a new era with Mike Macdonald as head coach and Sam Darnold signed up at quarterback following his career-defining year with the Minnesota Vikings in 2024. The faces on the sidelines and the names on the backs of the jerseys might have changed, but the same demands will be made by Seahawks fans, who have become used to watching a physical and successful team on Sundays.

HOME

LUMEN FIELD
Following the world's largest implosion of a concrete structure, Lumen Field was built on the site of the old Kingdome and opened for NFL play in 2002. Its modern design features high-banking stands that harness the noise created by Seahawks fans, who are known as the '12s', because they are considered the team's 12th man on the field. The 68,740-seat venue features an open north end, offering amazing views of downtown Seattle.

HEAD COACH

MIKE MACDONALD
The Seahawks are led by Mike Macdonald, who has worked his way through the American football coaching ranks, beginning at the high-school level in 2008. After a spell at college football's University of Georgia, Macdonald joined the Baltimore Ravens as an intern in 2014 and spent seven seasons with the AFC North club, rising to the position of linebackers coach. After working as defensive coordinator at the University of Michigan in 2021, Macdonald returned to oversee Baltimore's playmaking defense for two years. When hired by the Seahawks in January 2024, Macdonald became the NFL's youngest head coach at 36, and he delivered 10 wins in a promising first season.

SAM DARNOLD – QUARTERBACK

The Seahawks are led by a player who had been written off by many NFL experts in quarterback Sam Darnold. Chosen third overall by the New York Jets in 2018, Darnold entered the NFL with huge expectations. But he struggled badly in the Big Apple, once openly admitting during a game that he was 'seeing ghosts', which is an American football term for imagining pressures or coverages that are simply not there. After three seasons with the Jets, two with the Carolina Panthers and one with the San Francisco 49ers, Darnold was considered little more than a reserve option when he joined the Minnesota Vikings in 2024. But he enjoyed a career year subbing for the injured J.J. McCarthy, throwing for a career-high 4,319 yards and 35 touchdowns while leading his team to the playoffs. Darnold delivered many incredible throws in that 14-win campaign and grew as a leader. The all-star passer said: 'I learned a ton when I was a young player in the NFL. Yes, things didn't necessarily go my way all the time, but those are things I've been able to learn from.' Darnold signed a three-year deal with the Seahawks in March 2025 that was worth $100.5 million.

WALTER JONES – OFFENSIVE TACKLE

Any conversation about the greatest offensive linemen in NFL history simply must see one name go near the top of the list . . . Walter Jones – the man mountain left tackle who protected the blindside of Seattle quarterbacks for 12 seasons. Jones starred from 1997–2008, earning nine Pro Bowl trips. He was named to the NFL's All-Decade Team for the 2000s and took up his rightful place in the Pro Football Hall of Fame in 2014. During Jones' 180 straight starts in Seattle, Seahawks quarterbacks threw a total of 5,500 passes. Jones gave up just 23 sacks – or one for every 239 passes thrown! And he also gave up just nine holding penalties in his legendary career, proving he didn't need to bend the rules to succeed. Former Seahawks head coach Mike Holmgren labelled Jones: 'The best offensive player I ever coached.' It should be noted that Holmgren coached Hall of Fame quarterbacks such as Brett Favre, Joe Montana and Steve Young. Jones said of his career: 'I'm very proud of the offensive lines we built in Seattle. I want to say to the guys I went to battle with, our relationships mean so much to me to this day.'

MOMENT IN TIME

BEASTQUAKE!

In the 2010 season playoffs, Seahawks running back Marshawn 'Beast Mode' Lynch not only scored on one of the most spectacular touchdown runs in NFL history – the all-star sparked celebrations so wild that they registered as an earthquake in the city of Seattle. The Seahawks may have been playing at home, but they were big underdogs against the New Orleans Saints. Seattle led by four points with under four minutes remaining when Lynch set off downfield, breaking through and throwing off eight different Saints defenders before diving into the end zone to complete what was, figuratively and literally, a seismic 67-yard run. With the game won in that historic moment, Seahawks fans exploded into frenzied celebrations, jumping up and down and creating an earthquake that was tracked by the Pacific Northwest Seismic Network at the University of Washington and could be felt outside the stadium at the time. Then-Seahawks head coach Pete Carroll said: 'The stadium was just throbbing and it was one of the great moments I can remember.' Lynch's teammate and running back partner Justin Forsett summed up the atmosphere in Seattle that night when he admitted: 'It was so loud that your ears were still ringing after the game.'

★ DID YOU KNOW? ★

Seattle Seahawks defensive coordinator Aden Durde hails from London and previously worked for NFL UK and NFL International before moving to the Dallas Cowboys and now the Seahawks. The former linebacker played in NFL Europe for the Scottish Claymores and Hamburg Sea Devils and was a practice squad player for the Carolina Panthers.

TAMPA BAY BUCCANEERS

FIRST SEASON
1976

DIVISION
NFC South

COLOURS
Buccaneer red, pewter, orange and black

OWNERS
Bryan, Joel and Edward Glazer

HEAD COACH
Todd Bowles

STADIUM
Raymond James Stadium (69,218)

NFL TITLES/SUPER BOWLS:
2 **(2002, 2020)**

INTRODUCING THE BUCCANEERS . . .

The Tampa Bay Buccaneers have proven themselves to be an incredible, rags-to-riches tale. Their start in life in the NFL could not have been worse. The Bucs set a dubious record in 1976 by becoming the first team to record zero wins and 14 losses. By dropping their first 12 games of 1977, the Buccaneers entered the NFL with 26 soul-destroying defeats in a row.

Then-head coach John McKay – who won four national championships in college football – was asked by a reporter: 'How do you feel about your team's execution?' McKay paused for a moment then famously replied: 'Personally, I'm all for it!'

The Buccaneers found their footing and advanced to the NFC Championship Game in the 1979 season, kick-starting three playoff visits in four years. But the barren times returned as Tampa Bay failed to reach the knockout tournament every year from 1983 to 1986.

Super Bowl success finally came in 2002 – a season powered by one of the most dominant defenses in NFL history. And, in 2020, a second title was added following the inspired signing of legendary quarterback Tom Brady, who lifted the Vince Lombardi Trophy for the seventh time at the end of his first year in Tampa.

Brady is now retired and in the commentary booth, but the Buccaneers remain contenders with inspirational quarterback Baker Mayfield and ever-reliable wide receivers Mike Evans and Chris Godwin leading the way. They have reached the playoffs in each of the last five seasons and have won four NFC South titles in a row.

RAYMOND JAMES STADIUM
Raymond James Stadium opened in 1998 and features a full-sized pirate ship above one of the end zones, complete with cannons that fire in celebration and support of the home team. The 69,218-seat venue has played host to three Super Bowls, including in the 2020 season, when the Bucs became the first team to play in a Super Bowl in their own stadium.

TODD BOWLES
Todd Bowles is a former safety who played with Washington and then the San Francisco 49ers from 1986 to 1992. The no-nonsense leader has enjoyed success on and off the field. He won Super Bowl 22 as a player with Washington during the 1987 season. Bowles won another Super Bowl in 1996 as a member of the Green Bay Packers' personnel department. And he picked up a third Super Bowl ring as an assistant coach with the Bucs in 2020. Bowles, who led the New York Jets from 2015–2018, took charge of Tampa Bay in 2022 and has delivered three successive division crowns.

MIKE EVANS – WIDE RECEIVER

Mike Evans has been the picture of consistency and the model professional in more than a decade with the Tampa Bay Buccaneers. In each of his first 11 seasons, the Harry Potter-loving wide receiver chosen seventh in the 2014 NFL Draft has topped 1,000 receiving yards – the benchmark for leading receivers in the NFL. No other receiver in league history has achieved such a feat. The Texas native is one of the biggest wide receivers in NFL history at 6-foot-5 and 225 pounds. Evans is the complete package, because when the five-time all-star opens up his long stride, he blows past defensive backs and makes leaping catches downfield. Speaking of his remarkable consistency and dedication, the owner of every meaningful receiving record in Bucs' history said: 'Never get complacent. There's always something that you can get better at and just be a student of the game.' Evans was the youngest player in NFL history to reach 6,000 receiving yards, achieving that goal at the age of 25. He was also the fastest to 7,000 receiving yards at the age of 26. Now in year 12, the 32-year-old shows no signs of slowing down and remains one of the best in the business.

RONDE BARBER – CORNERBACK

The defense that drove Tampa Bay to glory in Super Bowl 37 featured several all-time greats. Among them was Hall of Fame cornerback Ronde Barber, who was chosen in the third round of the 1997 NFL Draft. In 16 seasons – all spent in Tampa Bay – Barber proved himself to be the epitome of class, consistency and playmaking versatility. Barber not only shadowed the opposing team's best receivers with supreme skill, he also displayed a nose for the football. Barber retired as the only defender in NFL history with more than 45 interceptions and 25 sacks. By the time he hung up his boots, the five-time all-star had 47 interceptions and had taken the quarterback down 28 times. His ability to turn those interceptions and 12 career fumble recoveries into something special was the stuff of legend. Barber scored 14 touchdowns during a glittering career – the most non-offensive touchdowns in Bucs history.

THE MOST UNIQUE OF HOME GAMES

On 7 February 2021, the Tampa Bay Buccaneers wrapped up the 2020 season with a home game that will never be forgotten in Super Bowl 55. The Bucs became the first team in league history to play in a Super Bowl in their own stadium as they took on the Kansas City Chiefs. That would have been notable enough. But this was also a Super Bowl played in the midst of global Covid-19-related lockdowns. That meant only 25,000 fans, including more than 7,000 healthcare workers, were able to attend the big game in person, and the rest of the Raymond James Stadium 'crowd' was made up of cardboard cut-out humans strategically positioned in seats across the venue. After a week of media commitments carried out on Zoom, the Buccaneers dominated on their way to a 31-9 victory. Tom Brady threw three touchdown passes, while his opposite number, Kansas City's Patrick Mahomes, was pressured from start to finish, being sacked three times, intercepted twice and held without a touchdown throw. On a special night in Florida, Brady became the oldest quarterback to start a Super Bowl at the age of 43. He was also named Most Valuable Player of the big game for a fifth time.

★ DID YOU KNOW? ★

After holding a name-the-team competition in 1975, Tampa Bay adopted their Buccaneers nickname as a reference to the pirates who frequently raided Florida's Gulf Coast in the 17th, 18th and 19th centuries. Then-owner Hugh Culverhouse selected the winning name with help from a panel of local journalists after receiving more than 400 alternative suggestions.

WASHINGTON COMMANDERS

FIRST SEASON
1932

OWNER
Josh Harris

DIVISION
NFC East

HEAD COACH
Dan Quinn

COLOURS
Burgundy, gold, white and black

STADIUM
Northwest Stadium (62,000)

NFL TITLES/SUPER BOWLS:
5 (1937, 1942, 1982, 1987, 1991)

INTRODUCING THE COMMANDERS . . .

The Commanders were formed in Boston in 1932 before moving to America's capital, Washington D.C., in 1937. The winners of more than 600 games and five NFL titles are as much a part of the Washington scene as those who have occupied the world's biggest seat of power in the White House.

Led by Hall of Fame quarterback 'Slingin' Sammy Baugh, Washington twice won NFL championships before the Super Bowl was born, in 1937 and 1942. And in the league's modern era – under the leadership of legendary head coach Joe Gibbs – Washington won three Super Bowls with three different quarterbacks in Joe Theismann (1982 season), Doug Williams (1987) and Mark Rypien (1991).

Washington fell on hard times from 2017 to 2023, failing to register a winning record in seven consecutive seasons. During that difficult period, the NFC East club rolled through 13 different quarterbacks, failing to find a long-term answer for the NFL's most important position. The good times returned in 2024 thanks to the arrival of sensational rookie quarterback Jayden Daniels. Washington won 12 regular season contests and beat Tampa Bay and Detroit in the playoffs before falling to the eventual-champion, the Philadelphia Eagles, in the NFC Championship Game.

With maturity beyond his 24 years and with breathtaking playmaking ability, Daniels has not only ignited belief in his teammates, he has given an entire city reason to dream of Super Bowl success that has not been seen in more than 30 years.

HOME

NORTHWEST STADIUM

The Commanders have played at their current home since 1997, when it opened on the site of an old dairy farm in Landover, Maryland – nine miles east of Washington D.C. – and named after former team owner Jack Kent Cooke. From 2004–2010, the venue was the largest in the NFL, seating 91,000 fans. The current capacity is 67,617. The venue has hosted many music and sporting events, including New Zealand's All Blacks beating USA 104-14 in a rugby union international in 2021.

HEAD COACH

DAN QUINN

The Commanders are led by one of American football's best motivators in 55-year-old Dan Quinn, who is in his second stint as an NFL head coach. Quinn entered the NFL as a defensive assistant with the San Francisco 49ers in 2001. After roles with the Miami Dolphins, New York Jets and Seattle Seahawks, he was named head coach of the Atlanta Falcons in 2015 and took his team to Super Bowl 51 in the 2016 season. Quinn was fired in 2020 and led one of the NFL's best defenses in the Dallas Cowboys before taking charge of Washington in 2024, immediately leading his new team to the playoffs. Quinn preaches strong relationships and a sense of brotherhood among his players, and delivers that message with great energy.

JAYDEN DANIELS – QUARTERBACK

Jayden Daniels wasted no time in announcing himself on the NFL stage in 2024, immediately turning the Commanders into a contender with his skilful throwing and fast and elusive running. Daniels played five seasons of college football at Arizona State and Louisiana State University, winning the prestigious Heisman Trophy (awarded to college football's best player) in 2023. After honing his skills by training for hundreds of hours while wearing virtual reality headsets, Daniels was polished and ready for the big leagues by the time he arrived in Washington as the second overall pick in the 2024 NFL Draft. During his rookie year, Daniels took the Commanders to within 60 minutes of the Super Bowl and displayed a complete array of skills, from arm strength and accuracy to an ability to evade defenders thanks to outstanding athleticism. The bigger the stage, the better he seems to play. The finest moment of Daniels' rookie campaign came in a Week 8 win over the Chicago Bears. Trailing by three points with just two seconds remaining, Daniels – who was playing with a rib injury – ran around for 12.79 seconds before heaving a 'Hail Mary' desperation pass more than 60 yards downfield for a Noah Brown touchdown and a famous 18-15 victory. A star was born! Daniels was named NFL Offensive Rookie of the Year for the 2024 season.

DARRELL GREEN – CORNERBACK

Darrell Green was the ultimate one-club player, starring for Washington for 20 seasons from 1983 to 2002. The cornerback voted to seven all-star games was blessed with blazing speed, which meant he could shadow the league's best receivers for two decades. The fastest official time recorded by an NFL player for a 40-yard sprint is 4.21 seconds by Kansas City wide receiver Xavier Worthy at the 2024 Combine. Green – a four-time winner of the NFL's Fastest Man sprint competition – clocked an unofficial time of 4.09 seconds during Washington's preseason camp in 1986, according to team insiders. By the time he retired at the age of 42, Green had recorded 54 interceptions and returned six of those steals for touchdowns. Those numbers would have been much higher had Green not been so great – there were long periods of games and seasons where opposing quarterbacks were simply too afraid to throw the ball in his direction. Green won two Super Bowls with Washington in 1987 and 1991 and was inducted into the Pro Football Hall of Fame after playing in a club record 295 games, proving himself to be the epitome of excellence, longevity and loyalty during a memorable career.

MOMENT IN TIME

THE SECOND QUARTER!

Doug Williams made history in the 1987 season, as he became the first African-American quarterback to start in a Super Bowl. In a testing week for the journeyman, Williams was peppered with questions about his ethnicity and was infamously asked: 'How long have you been a Black quarterback?' In the biggest game of his life, the 32-year-old Williams hurt his ankle in the first quarter and by the end of that 15 minutes, Washington trailed the Denver Broncos 10-0. Things looked bleak for Washington and their trail-blazing quarterback. But Williams had spent his whole sporting life fighting for respect and he was never going to limp out of Super Bowl 22. After that terrible opening quarter, Williams needed just 15 minutes to win the game and secure American football immortality. In just 18 plays, Washington scored 35 points and racked up more than 350 yards in a devastating explosion. Williams threw four touchdown passes in a record-setting quarter and ended the game with 340 passing yards in a 42-10 win. Williams was named the game's Most Valuable Player and, more importantly, changed the way NFL coaches and executives viewed Black quarterbacks, paving the way for the stars who dominate the league today.

★ DID YOU KNOW? ★

British defensive end Efe Obada, who played just five games of amateur American football with the London Warriors before entering the NFL as a practice squad player with the Dallas Cowboys in 2015, joined the Washington Commanders in 2022. Obada has also played for the Carolina Panthers and Buffalo Bills.

Glossary

GLOSSARY OF TERMS

You now know much more about the NFL and the sport of American football, but the chances are that you are going to hear a phrase or two that might not be familiar. When that happens, we've got you covered with our glossary of American football terms.

AUDIBLE
A last-second change from the play already called in the huddle. The quarterback shouts in code to change the play at the line.

BACKFIELD
The area behind the line of scrimmage, from where the quarterback will throw the football or the running back will start running the ball downfield.

BOMB
A long pass downfield.

BLITZ
An aggressive defensive play that sees more than the normal four defensive linemen go after the quarterback. Designed to hurry the quarterback into a mistake.

BOOTLEG
A deceptive move by the quarterback as he fakes giving the ball to the running back, keeps it and moves towards the sideline, from where he can either run himself or throw.

BUMP AND RUN
A defensive technique in which the cornerback hits the receiver at the line and then turns and runs downfield with him. He can only touch the receiver within five yards of the line of scrimmage.

CADENCE
The coded words the quarterback will shout at the line of scrimmage that will signal when the ball should be snapped to him by the center.

CHAIN
The 10-yard-long chain that is on the sideline and used to determine if an offense has gained the required yards for a fresh set of downs.

CUT
The term used to describe a player changing direction on the pitch.

DEFENSIVE BACKS
The collective name for the group of defenders who primarily cover the pass – cornerbacks and safeties.

GLOSSARY OF TERMS

DIME
A defensive formation in which a sixth defensive back is brought onto the field in passing situations.

DOWN
The term for a play that is run by the offense. The attacking team has four downs to move the ball 10 yards and gain a fresh set of downs.

DRAW
A fake pass that ends up being a run. The quarterback drops to pass and the linemen start backing up and blocking as if to protect for a throw, then the quarterback hands the ball to a runner instead.

END ZONE
The area 10 yards deep at each end of the field. Teams must get the ball into this area or catch a ball in this area to score a touchdown.

FACE MASK
The protective part of the helmet covering a player's face. If a defender grabs this while making a tackle, you will hear officials call a face mask penalty, which costs a defense 15 yards.

FAIR CATCH
When a player chooses not to risk returning a punt, he can wave his hand in the air and signal a fair catch. He cannot be interfered with at that time but must catch the ball to start his team's next possession at that spot.

FALSE START
A five-yard penalty called on the offense if a player moves before the snap of the ball.

FIELD GOAL
When the ball is kicked over the crossbar and between the posts, this is worth three points.

FLAG
When the yellow duster has been thrown to the ground, a foul has been committed.

FLEA FLICKER
A trick play where the quarterback hands the ball to

GLOSSARY OF TERMS

the running back, who moves towards the line as if on a normal rushing play. The running back then stops, tosses the ball back to the quarterback, who throws downfield, hopefully over the heads of defensive backs who have moved up to tackle the running back.

FRONT SEVEN
The first two lines of a defense are made up of defensive linemen and linebackers and is collectively known as the front seven. It will typically be three linemen and four linebackers or four linemen and three linebackers.

FUMBLE
A ball carrier loses possession of the ball. Any player on either team can recover a fumble.

HAIL MARY
A desperation pass used at the end of a half or a game. The quarterback throws the ball as high and as far as he can and then offers up a prayer, hence the name!

HAND-OFF
The passing of the ball from the quarterback to the running back on a rushing play.

HARD COUNT
When a quarterback deliberately changes his cadence ('hut, HUT, hut' for example) to try to get defenders to jump offside.

HASH MARKS
The two sets of lines running down the middle of the field that are used for spotting the ball. If the previous play ends outside the left hashmarks, it is set on the left line. Outside the right, it is set on the right hashmarks. Wherever a previous play ends within the hashmarks is where the next play begins.

HOLE
The space opened by blockers for the ball carrier.

HUDDLE
The brief gathering between plays to decide who does what next.

GLOSSARY OF TERMS

HURRY-UP OFFENSE
When a team needs to score quickly, they will likely not huddle up and will operate a hurry-up offense with the quarterback shouting coded plays to his teammates to save time.

ICING THE KICKER
If a kicker is lining up for an important or winning kick, the opposing team will call a time out in an attempt to 'ice' and put off the kicker by delaying the game.

INSTANT REPLAY
The TV replay system used to settle disputed plays. Coaches can throw red challenge flags to set up replay reviews. All touchdowns and turnovers are automatically reviewed.

INTENTIONAL GROUNDING
Quarterbacks are not allowed to deliberately throw the ball into the ground to avoid being tackled for a sack. The passer can throw the ball away if they have moved wider than the offensive tackles.

INTERCEPTION
A pass that is caught by a member of the defense.

LATERAL
A backward pass like those seen in rugby, although they are much less common in the NFL.

LINE OF SCRIMMAGE
The imaginary line where each play begins, with the offensive and defensive lines facing off against each other. Defenders are not allowed to move across the line of scrimmage until the ball is snapped. All measurements for first downs relate back to the line of scrimmage.

MAN COVERAGE
A defensive approach that sees the cornerbacks mark the wide receivers man for man, following them wherever they go on the field.

GLOSSARY OF TERMS

MOTION
The movement of a player – a wide receiver, tight end or running back – from one side of the formation to the other before the snap. Designed to either create mismatches or to discover how the defense is covering the play

MUFF
When a player drops a punt and the ball is free on the ground for both teams to gather.

NICKEL
A defense in which a fifth defensive back is brought onto the field in a passing situation.

OFFSIDE
A penalty called on a defender if he crosses the line of scrimmage before the ball is snapped.

ONSIDE KICK
A short, bouncing kick designed to get the ball back for the kicking team after it has travelled 10 yards. Used in desperate situations when a team is trailing. Under new kick-off rules, teams must announce when they are going to attempt an onside kick.

PASS INTERFERENCE
Defensive backs are not allowed to touch or hinder a receiver's chance to catch the football once it is in the air. If a penalty occurs, the ball is spotted at the point of the foul.

PASS RUSH
Refers to the pressure a defense puts on the quarterback on a passing play. Players who perform this task – regardless of their position – are known as pass rushers.

PICK SIX
An interception – which can also be referred to as a pick – that is returned by the defender for a touchdown, worth six points.

PITCH
An underhand toss of the ball to the running back on rushing plays.

PLAY ACTION PASS
A deceptive play. The quarterback pretends to hand

GLOSSARY OF TERMS

the ball to the running back, pulls it back at the last second and throws downfield, again looking to expose defenders who have moved up to take on a running play.

POCKET
The area around the quarterback formed by his blockers as he drops back to pass.

PUNT
A fourth down kick for territory when an offense has failed to pick up a new set of downs.

RED ZONE
The area of the field from the 20-yard line in. Nothing is painted red on the field, it is just referred to as the red zone because it is the most important area for scoring or stopping a team from scoring.

REVERSE
An offensive play in which a receiver or running back will run in one direction and hand the ball to another player coming the other way. Designed to fool

the defense into giving up big yardage.

RUN-PASS OPTION
An offensive play in which the quarterback reads a defender and, depending on what he sees, he will decide at the last second to give the ball to the running back for a run or keep the ball himself and throw downfield.

SACK
A big play for the defense! The quarterback is tackled for a loss when attempting to throw.

SAFETY
American football's own goal! When a player is tackled in his own end zone, it's two points for the other team.

SCRAMBLE
A quarterback improvises and runs to evade pressure or pick up yardage.

SCREEN PASS
A short throw to either the running back or, more increasingly, the wide receiver,

GLOSSARY OF TERMS

who will then run behind a wall of blockers who have moved to his side of the field while the ball was in the air.

SCRIMMAGE YARDS
The yardage accrued by a player in a game or season through both running the football and catching passes.

SHOTGUN
An offensive formation that sees the quarterback stood five yards from the line, allowing for additional time to throw.

SNAP
The passing of the ball from the center to the quarterback, which starts every play.

SWEEP
A run around one end of the line.

TOUCHDOWN
The most valuable score in American football, worth six points.

TURNOVER
The collective name for an interception or fumble that is recovered by the defense.

YAC
This is a vital component of any attack and stands for 'Yards After Catch'. It refers to the yardage gained by a ball-carrier after he has made a catch.

ZEBRAS
The nickname for the striped-shirt wearing officials, of which there are seven in every game.

ZONE DEFENSE
The alternative to playing man coverage. The defenders cover certain areas of the field rather than following receivers and running backs man to man. The American football equivalent of the zonal marking we see on free kicks and corners in football.

ACKNOWLEDGEMENTS

Despite the 14-year-old version of me once being told by a school careers advisor that 'journalism would be too hard and too competitive' and that I 'might want to consider another line of work', I'm somehow approaching 30 years of covering my sporting passion – that is, American football and its premier league, the NFL.

Like the rest of my career, writing this book has been a truly rewarding experience, and it would not have been possible without the support, insight and encouragement of many individuals – all of whom either share my love for this incredible sport or recognise that I have an NFL 'sickness' that will never be cured.

I would like to thank my colleagues at Sky Sports and NFL UK – past and present – for creating a platform where storytelling and passion for the game is encouraged and celebrated, every week of each and every season. Those colleagues and that environment has given me countless wonderful experiences and made every early-morning alarm call, every trans-Atlantic flight and every 'way-too-late' finish worth it.

I would also like to extend heartfelt thanks to the many players, coaches and executives who have generously given their time, sharing their stories and insights with me over the years. There are far too many to list, of course, but their contributions to this and many other projects have always been and will always be appreciated.

However, I would like to extend special thanks to NFL Academy head coach Steve Hagen for his assistance on the 'Advanced Tactics' section of this book. There is great work being done by Coach Hagen and his staff in Loughborough, helping to shape young student athletes and sending many of them on their way to the American university system, and even to the NFL.

I would like to offer special thanks to Samuel Heaton at Penguin too, who came to me with the idea that our bookshop shelves were sorely missing an international guide to what used to be the most American

ACKNOWLEDGEMENTS

of sports. But with a publication of this nature, it is always difficult for an NFL anorak like myself to pitch the information at the right level. I wanted this book to be interesting to existing fans but also accessible to those new to the NFL. Sam's job was to keep me honest, to question and to challenge at every necessary turn, and to stop me from getting too deep into the technical weeds. I am also very happy to report that Sam's own fandom of the NFL has grown through the course of this project, even though I am worried he is shaping up to be a New England Patriots fan!

Most importantly, I want to thank my family, starting with my children – George, Daisy and Poppy. I love you all so much and I'm so proud that each of you has grown up to be a good and caring person with a strong work ethic and an ambitious and energetic approach to life. And I absolutely love the fact that our entire household enjoys this shared passion and lives and breathes the NFL. *Every* day is an American football day in our house, not just Sundays!

To my wife, Julie . . . thank you for your patience and continued love and support throughout my decades covering the NFL. There is no doubt that the NFL calendar is relentless, which is probably why we so often use the phrase 'There is no offseason.' I miss more than my fair share of weekends, school runs, family get-togethers and quiet evenings at home, and I don't think many of our household bills would get paid if it were left up to me. Thank you for being the absolute rock of our family, for being our head coach, and for letting me chase this and many other NFL-related dreams.

Finally, thanks to you, the fans. Whether you have followed the NFL for 30 years or 30 days, this is for you. Your growing passion for the NFL has allowed me to write this book. That is something I could not have dreamed of doing when I first started pinning Dan Marino posters to my bedroom wall in the 1980s. I hope you enjoy it!

The quotes in this book come from Neil's interviews with key figures from the NFL except for the following quotes: Page 47, Mike McCarthy Press Conference, 2022; Page 50, Daniel Jeremiah quote from NFL.com; Page 55 Lamar Jackson quote from Tenessee titans.com, October 15 2023, 'QB Lamar Jackson'; Page 55 Tom Brady quote from NFL.com, November 13 2022, 'Tom Brady leads Buccaneers to victory in Munich'; Page 58, Mark Sanchez quote from ESPN, November 28 2012, 'Mark Sanchez discusses fumble'; Page 58 Rex Ryan quote from ESPN, November 22

ACKNOWLEDGEMENTS

2022, 'Long Live the Butt Fumble'; Page 58, Carnell Lake quote from The Athletic, November 23 2023, 'The Lions, the Steelers and a crazy, botched Thanksgiving coin flip 25 years ago'; Page 59, Mike Tomlin quote from ESPN, November 25 2020, 'A Thanksgiving trip'; Page 59, Brad Smith quote from ESPN, November 26, 2020, 'Mr Smith goes to the end zone, twice'; Page 90, Sam Wyche, Press Conference; Page 96, Sam Huff quote taken from Neil's previous book Pain Gang (2006); Page 97, Mike Brown quote from The New York Times, September 25 1997, 'When Paul Brown Smashed the Colour Barrier'; Page 103, John Elway quote from Denver Broncos YouTube, October 22, 2022, John Elway recreates 'The Helicopter'; Page 109, Andre Johnson quote from New York Post, January 8 2012, 'Texans defeat Bengals'; Page 113, Kwity Paye quote from NFL Network (Top 100 Players of 2024); Page 131, Maxx Crosby quote from NFL Network (Top 100 Players of 2024); Page 131, Terron Armstead quote from NFL Network (Top 100 Players of 2024); Page 133, Ron Wolf quote from NFL Films; Page 137, Jim Harbaugh quote from The Herd with Colin Cowherd, 17 June 2023; Page 149, Sean McVay quote from Yahoo Sports, November 18 2024, 'Sean McVay impressed with Drake Maye'; Page 151, Tom Brady quote from NFL Youtube, 'Superbowl LI: Patriots vs. Falcons Mic'd Up; Page 167, Jaylen Warren quote from NFL Films; Page 168, Ed O'Neil quote taken from Neil's previous book Pain Gang (2006); Page 188, Tony Dungy quote taken from Panthers.com, August 02 2024, 'Hall of Famers praise Julius Peppers as "old-school player in a new type of body" '; Page 189, John Fox quote from Panthers.com, July 09 2019, '25 seasons of Panthers Football'; Page 194, Jack Youngblood quote taken from Neil's previous book Pain Gang (2006); Page 198, Jerry Jones quote from BleacherReport.com, Febuary 8 2025, 'Cowboys' Jerry Jones Explains Thought Process Behind Brian Schottenheimer Hire as HC'; Page 200, Bill Belichick quote from USAToday.com, 2019, 'Bill Belichick floored Emmitt Smith with the ultimate compliment'; Page 201, Tom Landry quote from Dallas Cowboys.com, November 08 2019, 'A Pass and a Prayer'; Page 201, Roger Staubach quote from Dallas Cowboys.com, November 08 2019, 'A Pass and a Prayer'; Page 207, Aidan Hutchinson quote from Sunday Night Football on NBC , 15 January 2024, 'Aidan Hutchinson was playing for his city and his teammates; Page 207, Jared Goff quote from ESPN.co.uk, January 15 2024, 'Jared Goff leads Lions to first playoff win in 32 years'; Page 213, Walt Garrison quote from

ACKNOWLEDGEMENTS

East Texas Journal, May 31 2018, 'Meredith's Son Lands NFL Film for Home Team'; Page 218, Sean McVay quote from CBS Sports, February 14 2022, 'LOOK: Rams' Sean McVay predicted Aaron Donald's play to seal Super Bowl 2022 win for Los Angeles'; Page 219, Mike Jones quote from Bleacher Report, February 2 2019, 'Where Are They Now? Mike Jones Made the Most Famous Tackle in Super Bowl History'; Page 229, Drew Brees quote from New York Times, December 25 2020, 'Alvin Kamara Runs for Six Touchdowns Against Vikings'; Page 236, John Randle quote from NFL.com, 'Linebacker Lawrence Taylor'; Page 237, David Tyree quote from Giants.com, February 3 2025, 'One Giant Victory'; Page 241, Nick Sirianni quote from NFL.com, November 04 2024, 'Eagles HC Nick Sirianni on Saquon Barkley's reverse leapfrog'; Page 242, Reggie White quote from NFL Youtube channel, June 11 2016, #7: Reggie White – The top 100: NFL's Greatest Players; Page 243, Nike Foles and Doug Pederson quote from CBS News, February 6 2018, 'Philly Philly'; Page 246, Joe Staley quote from NFL.com, January 25 2020, 'Kyle Shanahan . . . Greatest Play-Caller Ever?'; Page 255, Pete Carroll quote from NFL.com; Page 255, Justin Forsett quote from NFL. com, 'Marshawn Lynch "Beast Quake" Run Through Saints'.

ABOUT THE AUTHOR

Neil Reynolds is the presenter of the NFL on Sky Sports and has been at the forefront of American football's TV coverage in the United Kingdom since 2011, twice being short-listed for Sports Presenter of the Year awards. Prior to that, Neil worked as an NFL commentator and pundit on BBC Radio 5 Live for two years. A full-time journalist covering the NFL since 1997, Neil currently writes for NFL.com, SkySports.com and the official Super Bowl game programme sold in the United States, and serves as editor of the NFL's gameday programmes for matches in the UK and across Europe. Neil also works as a content creator and event host for NFL UK and NFL teams such as the Jacksonville Jaguars and New York Jets. Neil is the host of the Inside the Huddle podcast and also co-hosts the Extra Point podcast alongside fellow NFL enthusiasts Vernon Kay and Darren Fletcher.